the idea of
DELHI

the idea of
DELHI

Marg publications

edited by Romi Khosla

with photographs by Nitin Rai

General Editor
PRATAPADITYA PAL

Research Editor
ANNAPURNA GARIMELLA

Executive Editors
SAVITA CHANDIRAMANI
RIVKA ISRAEL

Editorial Executives
ARNAVAZ K. BHANSALI
L.K. MEHTA

Senior Production Executive
GAUTAM V. JADHAV

Production Executive
VIDYADHAR R. SAWANT

Design
KIRTI TRIVEDI

Vol. 56 No. 3
March 2005
Price: Rs 2500.00 / US$ 66.00
ISBN: 81-85026-69-6
Library of Congress Catalog
Card Number: 2005-318064

Marg is a registered trademark
of Marg Publications
© Marg Publications, 2005
All rights reserved

Published by J.J. Bhabha
for Marg Publications on behalf of
the National Centre for the
Performing Arts at
24, Homi Mody Street,
Mumbai 400 001.

Colour and black and white
processing by Reproscan,
Mumbai 400 013.

Printed by A.S. Vadiwala at
Infomedia India Limited, Nerul,
Navi Mumbai 400 706, India.

Contents

Marg Publications gratefully acknowledges the generous support
extended by UTI Bank in the publication of this volume.

UTI BANK
Solutions for a lifetime

Romi Khosla

The City as an Idea

This book is about the imagined conceptions of Delhi and how its rulers have tried to convert these ideas into urban reality. Before the republican era began, Delhi was ruled by monarchs and emperors. With the end of the feudal order and the beginnings of independence and the democratic experiment, the rulers became the elected representatives and their vote banks. Through every period of change, continuity was provided by the bureaucracies which exercised control on the implementation process that transformed the various rulers' concepts into built form. The cord that runs through the chapters of the book is composed primarily with conceptions of Delhi, emphasizing more the intellectual pursuits of making a capital rather than documenting its historical narrative. There has been much written about the histories that have layered this city, but less about the visions and ideas that its rulers have tried to realize in laying out the cityscape. These ideas and visions were often first given physical form through geometry. Geometry was one of the crucial tools to map and implement heavenly ideals on earth. These urban geometries served to determine the patterns that have woven together the cores and peripheries of the planned city, rather like the geometric design in a woven carpet that is laid out in all its splendour before it is used and misused by the people who tred on it. Beneath the dust and footprints that the inhabitants have left behind, the underlying sense of order that its rulers through the ages tried to give Delhi can still be discerned in the significant landmarks that dot the metropolis as monumental presences.

The influence of a predetermined concept on the layout of a city presumes not only that a concept is formulated prior to construction but also that the conceiver views the city as an object, a thing with finite components that serve to extend the existing power structure. The city could be viewed therefore as an abstract object of beauty as Shahjahan did, but also as a representation of the benevolence of its rulers. It is this object that all rulers seek to alter, improve, or idealize in some way. It is almost as if the rulers find it easier and quicker to idealize the container in which their subjects dwell, than to change or idealize the subjects themselves. Architectural gestures can be completed within the lifetime of the patron while social change takes much longer. The arrangement of open spaces, built forms, movement patterns, and social hierarchies are the chess pieces to regulate the order of the lives of the subjects. Primarily it is the order of law that regulates daily life in a city but the foundation of this consists of a well ordered urban geometry. Before the inhabitants are able to be regulated by the order of law, they need to be placed within a geometrically regulated urban fabric. The geometrical lines that are scratched on the site of the future city can be chosen for abstract reasons but they eventually have higher ideological reasons. For example, the geometric order of the planned city can reflect a Mughal emperor's wish to lay out the pattern of a garden of paradise on the city; or it can reflect a colonial ruler's insistence on the classical and

1 *opposite*
The urban geometry of colonial Delhi sought to place order in the heart of a disordered empire. Satellite image courtesy S.M. Chadha.

2
The Viceroy's House was placed at the head of the central axis of the King's Way. From a postcard, courtesy Anil Dave.

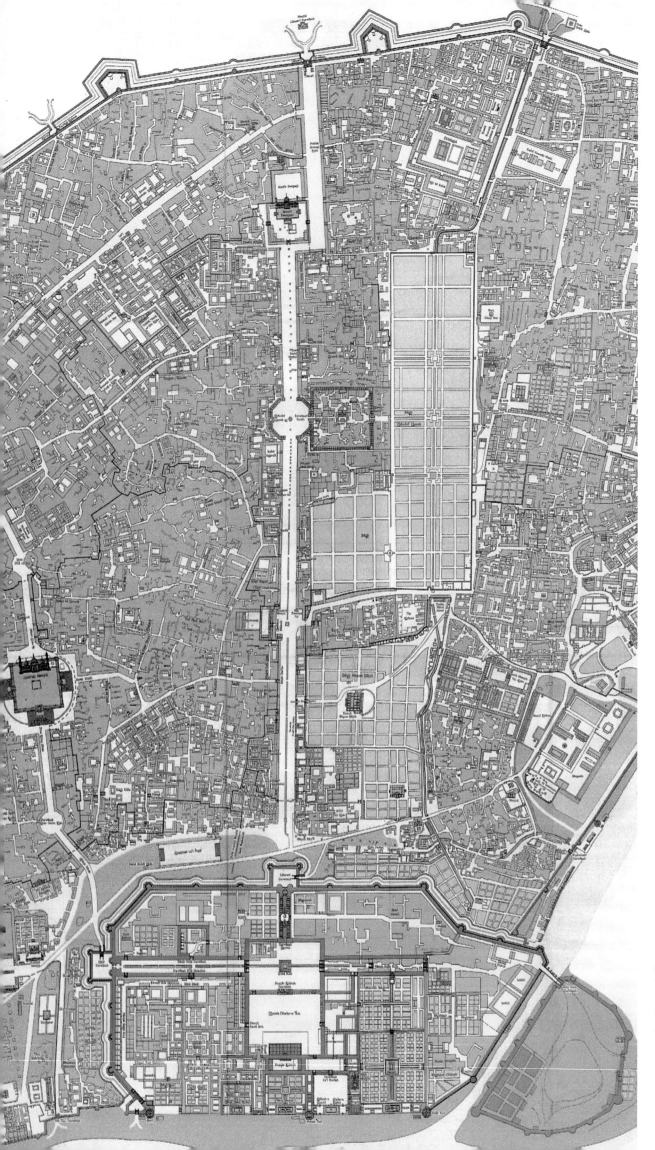

3
The urban geometry of
Mughal Delhi alluded to
the gardens of Central
Asia and Persia (detail of
map on pages 98–99).

Romi Khosla

imposing plan of wide boulevards to regulate habitation; or for that matter, it could be a reflection of a Le Corbusier choosing to pattern the city of the future on a grid iron geometry; or some anonymous planning department which ceaselessly bisects the land into plots for distribution to a land-hungry electorate.

The prescription of an ordered city for the harmonious living of citizens is evident in the urban layouts in some of the most ancient excavation sites. The origins of efforts to promote ideal urban centres and life can be traced back to various roots depending on one's cultural preferences. Some scholars are content to trace these origins to Plato who, it is claimed, first described the ideal city in *The Republic* which he wrote after Athens was defeated in 404 BCE. Generations of planners, particularly in the West, have been influenced by the platonic notion of an ideal and that the ideal social organization needs to be reared in some sort of an ideal urban setting. There are other scholars who claim entirely different roots which are traced to the Koran or some ancient Indian *shastra* or Chinese manual. Regardless of searching to authenticate one or the other source, it remains valid to contend that almost since its inception, the city has been regarded as an object that was moulded by its ruling authorities to impose order on its subjects and where citizen behaviour needed to be regulated tightly to preserve the status quo and aspire for some higher glorification of an ideal. It is only in the more recent closing decades of the last century that the city has begun to be regarded by planners as an organism with its own and unpredictable dynamism and where the pursuit of an ideal master plan has become a dated notion. The growth of democracy and the growing influence of the academia of the social sciences have produced a multitude of theoretical and empirical studies about the functioning of the city as an organism rather than a static ideal linked to cosmic design.

This process of shifting urban studies into the fold of the social sciences took time and did not impact notions of the city till the 1950s. Before that, while the theoretical formulation of the city remained strongly influenced by the notion of an ideal, it had been taken over by the influence of the Fabians and other pro-working-class thinkers who have been termed as the early visionaries. The advent of the Industrial Revolution and the rise of the industrial megalopolis provided the new idealized object to the visionary planners in the early 20th century. They continued to regard the city as a definable static object that could be idealized.

4 & 5
Chandni Chowk – the central axis of Mughal Delhi was always envisaged as a commercial street where the life of its citizens ebbed and flowed.

This was also the time when the British were beginning to conceive of a new imperial capital for India. The concepts for the layout of New Delhi were formed out of a congerie of ideas put forward by visionaries such as Patrick Geddes, Lewis Mumford, and Ebenezer Howard. Starting with the underlying assumption that the inhabitants of the growing industrial cities were suffering from diseases of social disorder caused by sudden industrialization, they argued for a vision of the ideal city which could cure these ills. Whereas Plato had ascribed the defeat in the Peloponnesian war to the social decay of Athens, the early 20th-century visionaries ascribed the urban unrest to the advent of the factory and the waves of migrations from the countryside during the Victorian era. The planners of New Delhi sought through the establishment of the imperial city to bring some order to the chaotic conditions of native life witnessed by British rulers within the quarters of Shahjahanabad – a place that had nursed the Revolt of 1857.

These visionaries had various concepts about the essential characteristic of an ideal city. Perhaps the most influential was the stenographer, Ebenezer Howard. He was obsessed with a passion for change. It was a passion that ceaselessly energized him to propagate his ideas in public. He first published his ideas in 1898 in a book titled *To-morrow: a Peaceful Path to Social Reform*. Four years later it was re-edited and published by its better known title *Garden Cities of Tomorrow*. Howard was a Fabian in his beliefs and strongly supported the cause of

6
The Red Fort palace of the Mughal Emperor, now a monument with a confused identity shared by the army, the Archaeological Survey, and tourist guides.

Romi Khosla

the Land Nationalisation Society. It is not a coincidence that almost the entire territory of what is called "Lutyens' Delhi" today consists of government-owned land. His utopian vision made him prominent among the handful of early socialist planners in Europe and America, almost all of whom held radical beliefs based on the assertion that human civilization had been corrupted by the greed of capitalism and that the process of industrialization had to be humanized by removing exploitation. For Howard, such humanity was to be restored to civilization through a re-formulation of the physical environment by moving away from Victorian cities and their slums to new sites scattered throughout the countryside. These sites would have finite sizes of population and planned layouts that restored the balance between built form and nature. The morphology for these cities was based on the idea of citizens perpetually living in a garden environment. Howard propagated his theories through public lectures that he illustrated with slides taken from his book. These illustrations captured the essence of his argument and served as summaries of the fuller explanations in his book. Often they were images overwritten with textual explanations. Perhaps one of the more well known of these images was the "Three Magnet" diagram which showed "The People" being attracted to two existing magnets – one the wretched polluted town and the other the jobless countryside. The third magnet to be introduced was the garden city which was both town and country and thus held the greatest attraction.

7
The fountains of Imperial Delhi with the offices of the bureaucracy in the background. The rulers of Independent India comfortably slipped into the Imperial shoes.

8
Chudi Bazar located inside the
bye-lanes of Shahjahanabad.

Howard's ideas influenced a wide range of his contemporaries who were engaged in one way or other in social engineering solutions to the evils of industrialization. Although his Fabian ideas for social reform were largely diluted if not ignored, his geometries and diagrams of the physical layout of garden cities lived on for decades. Industrial benefactors amongst the Quaker chocolate capitalists were among the first patrons of these garden cities. The early incomplete experimental attempts at building garden cities began in England in 1903 with the founding of Letchworth, to be followed by Bourneville, Hampstead Garden Suburb, Welwyn Garden City, and then a host of others in the decades that followed. The band of professional urban planners steadily increased in number. Much of the implementation and physical planning work of early garden cities was carried forward by Barry Parker, Raymond Unwin, and Louis de Soissons as architects who could give physical urban form to the ideas of Ebenezer Howard. Edwin Lutyens too was clearly influenced by the Garden City movement as the concept began to be implemented at various sites. He was appointed the consulting architect for the Hampstead Garden Suburb Trust in 1906 and his involvement with the Garden City movement was to have a profound impact on the physical planning of Delhi when he was appointed to the Delhi Town Planning Committee in 1912.

The immediate proximity of the Mughal capital presented a challenge to the British who had taken a political decision to move the capital from Calcutta to Delhi. It was a challenge that demanded a suitable response by an imperial power that regarded its grandeur as being far superior to that of the Mughals. There was a need to diminish the perceived grandeur of the Mughals in the eyes of the "natives" otherwise they would be difficult to rule. The 1857 Revolt had already demonstrated that the Indians would have preferred to restore Mughal rule. In terms of the physical layout of the city, Mughal monuments needed to be subjugated permanently and the Government House of the Viceroy had to be located higher than the minarets of the Jama Masjid in Shahjahanabad, created by the Mughal Emperor Shahjahan

Romi Khosla

(1627–58). Even the rich Persian and Central Asian architectural motifs in the palaces of the Mughals had to be supplanted with the "superior" architectural heritage of Greek and Roman classicism. This heritage needed to be encoded into the monumental facades of the key buildings that symbolized the power of the British Empire. For its rulers, New Delhi had to reflect the glory of their empire. This superiority was to be read on the surfaces of the buildings and was to consist of motifs that dipped eclectically into classical as well as modern times. Grand structures built in the classical forms of a superior civilization were to be laid out according to the latest town-planning principles.

The various settlements that have collectively been termed Delhi have always had importance as centres of the various territories that successive rulers had carved out in northern India. Delhi was strategically located on the fertile plains of the Yamuna river and its immediate hinterland was enclosed by the hills of the Southern Ridge. The triangular space formed between the southeastern flow of the Yamuna and the southwestern extension of the Ridge became a natural place for locating an urban settlement. The so-called seven (some count them as nine) Delhis are all located within this triangular plain. It is only the very recent suburban extensions such as NOIDA which has crossed the Yamuna to spread eastwards and Gurgaon that has come further south, which are outside the triangular plain.

Shahjahan's decision to locate a well-planned capital city on the banks of the river was made after he had been on the throne for a decade. His urban interventions made in Lahore and Agra preceded his founding of Shahjahanabad. The formality of the city's layout is evident in the 1850 map of the British administration (redrawn in the Department of Geography of the University of Bonn in 1992). The perfect formal geometrical layout was confined to the enclosed space within the red sandstone walls of the Red Fort citadel whose sides have been placed axially to the cardinal points. The city outside the citadel walls was not overlaid by any grid. Wherever simple rectilinear geometric spaces have been formally arranged, there is clearly a reference to the gardens of paradise whose features included a central water canal punctuated with cross water channels flowing towards the cardinal points. The urban morphology of the city is a mixture of formal and organic geometries and reflects the layouts of Persian towns, but more directly the Timurid and post-Timurid layouts of Central Asian cities such as Samarkand. For example, the location of Timur's citadel at one edge of the city wall has parallels in the siting of the Red Fort. Other Timurid features such as the grand avenue of shops leading to the citadel gates cutting across the urban fabric, and the location of the Registan square within the residential quarters of the city have clear parallels in the layout of the avenue of Chandni Chowk and the placement of Jama Masjid. Even though our reading of the urban morphology of Shahjahanabad is restricted to the 1850 map, nevertheless the Central Asian urban components that regulated the lives of the citizens are clearly apparent. Just as the colonial layout of New Delhi was intended to demonstrate the higher urban culture of a superior Western civilization, so Shahjahanbad was created to present to the people of India the higher and more ordered urban civilization of Timurid Central Asia.

All cities are made up of similar urban components. These consist of a system of open spaces (parks and gardens), commercial centres, a system of roads and avenues, residential quarters with their own local shopping facilities, and the inevitable monumental presence of the central cathedral of worship usually linked in some way to the palace of government. Each culture interprets and styles these components in its own unique way and Shahjahanabad was no exception to the rule. One is struck immediately by the elaborate canal system that was used to water the series of gardens landscaped at prime sites along Chandni Chowk. These canals were fed from the waters of the Yamuna that had been tapped, since pre-Shahjahan times, by a waterway some miles north of the city. This canal brought the river water to the western wall of the city, entering it at Kabul Gate. The canal irrigated the elaborate gardens

9
Jama Masjid, the
Friday mosque of
Mughal Delhi,
was embedded
into the kasba of
Shahjahanabad's
urban fabric.

Romi Khosla

that lay north of Chandni Chowk and acted as a central channel that divided Chandni Chowk. Its final destination was the citadel where the water flowed into elaborately laid out paradise gardens through a network of water channels and fountains. The city's gardens were designed in a hierarchy that began with the complex layout of the Red Fort gardens, then moving on to the simpler open public gardens such as those north of Chandni Chowk, and ending with the smaller individual gardens attached to public institutions that could not get the canal water and relied on a supply provided by the various step wells and spring wells that dotted the city.

Shahjahanabad's commercial streets were split into two separate bazaars. In the earlier Central Asian prototypes, these commercial streets often crossed each other at a chowk or *chor'su*. In some of the more formal city plans such as in Samarkand, Bokhara, and Khiva these bazaar streets crossed at the centre of the city, dividing the city into four quarters. In the case of Shahjahanabad, the main artery of Chandni Chowk with its 1,500 shops stretched from the Fatehpuri Masjid to Lahore Gate. The second, less important commercial avenue with half as many shops, known today as Daryaganj, stretched from Delhi Gate to the city walls. A third winding commercial avenue linked the fort to the Jama Masjid which, like its Timurid counterparts, was placed in the midst of the residential mohallas whose urban fabric was built virtually up to its external walls. The Friday prayer mosque was meant to be revealed suddenly in its grandeur as one wound one's way towards it along the narrow streets of the mohallas. Unlike the fort, the main mosque was not meant to be beheld as a stand-alone monument from a distance.

In 1803, a century and a half after Shahjahan took charge of Delhi, the British administrators of Delhi took charge of Shahjahanabad. They more or less left its Mughal morphology undisturbed till 1858 when the acts of vengeance by the new British rulers on the rebellious inhabitants of Delhi were traumatic. There were large-scale demolitions carried out and a brutal system of urban clearances that were supposed to give the colonial army easy access to the various quarters of the city. Ironically this brutal action was carried out at the same time as Baron Haussmann was ripping Paris apart to gain access to the quarters that had become strongholds of the revolutions of 1830 and 1848. Haussmann destroyed over 15,000 homes in Paris to provide the city with its avenues and a better hygienic environment. Similarly in Shahjahanabad, the British administration demolished all the houses of the

10 & 11
Inlay and relief carving on the surface of Jama Masjid – a rich tapestry of decorative elements from Central Asian carpets.

12–15
NOIDA located in Uttar Pradesh has become a suburb of Delhi. Unlike Gurgaon, it has been developed by the government to provide plotted houses for the rising tide of retired officials.

Romi Khosla

important families in the proximity of the fort and converted the mohallas into a grassed parkland where today dutiful listeners squat each Independence Day and listen to the Prime Minister's speech.

But Shahjahanabad could not serve as the centre of power for the British administration. It was too densely populated and difficult to police. It took some five decades after 1857 for the colonial rulers to secure for themselves a safe and what was assumed to be a permanent empire on which the sun would never set. Then it was time for plans to be drawn up for the ultimate imperial capital that would herald a new era of Indian history. Calcutta, which was till 1911 the capital of India, was restless with what Lord Hardinge referred to as "undue Bengali influence upon members of the legislative assembly". So the site of New Delhi was decided upon as ideal, away from the seething populations of Calcutta but also removed from rebellious Shahjahanabad. There were other reasons for the transfer, both practical and symbolic: the historical importance of Delhi, the rising "terrorism and sedition" in Calcutta, the need to dissociate the commercial hub from political power, and the need to support the geographical expansion of the empire from the eastern coast to the heart of India. Delhi also had proximity to Simla the summer capital. However, before this great venture could be completed to gain the proportions of an imperial Roman gesture, the First World War intervened and diverted the silver in the coffers of the British treasury to armaments and away from empire building. New Delhi became the capital city in 1929. In the meantime the "seething Indians" had rapidly advanced their cause of freedom, and in less than two decades since its inception, Delhi witnessed independent India's leaders and bureaucrats walking down the corridors and occupying the rooms that the British had vacated in the imperial buildings of the great city of New Delhi.

As Indians began to occupy the spaces left behind by the British, so the streaming refugees from the newly created Pakistan began to occupy all the spaces left behind by the Muslim citizens of Delhi fleeing to Pakistan. (As a matter of interest, the present leader of Pakistan, General Musharraf was born in Old Delhi.) The migration of refugees from Pakistan was enormous and large tracts of land in the hinterland of Delhi began to be converted from agricultural use to housing plots. The idea of a city ideal began to be transformed from a "grand vision" to the "grand adjustment". Ironically, as Prime Minister Jawaharlal Nehru (1947–64) was briefing Le Corbusier about the future Chandigarh and the need for an ideal city to be the symbol of independent India, the capital city in which he sat was being mutated from a Mughal and a colonial ideal into a settlement of refugees which would render it an unknown place to its older inhabitants. The expanding boundaries of the urban geography of Delhi was on its way to accommodating a megapolis with a population of over ten million. At the time of the establishment of New Delhi, Shahjahanabad had a population of 233,000 living in an area of about 30 square kilometres. The New Delhi Lutyens plan was designed to extend across 52 square kilometres with an intended population of between 30,000 and 57,000. However, after Partition, within four years, almost 500,000 refugees had streamed into Delhi to more than replace the 330,000 Muslims who had migrated to Pakistan. In addition, Delhi's natural increase of population during those four years after Partition was just over 200,000. The brunt of the post-Partition pressure of population was taken by Shahjahanabad which was rapidly reduced to a large commercial cum residential slum. The space in Lutyens' Delhi was secured by government land. The migrants streamed to the periphery. The periphery of Delhi was thus transformed into plotted colonies by both private as well as government agencies, and the so-called cooperative societies. The refugees, the natural increase in the local population, as well as all the migrants from all other regions of the new nation who sought out Delhi for opportunities during the next five decades were accommodated in the "grand adjustment" that placed unlimited land at the disposal of developers – either private ones or thinly disguised as government agencies.

The notion that the entire city could be the ideal vehicle for social transformation could not be stretched across a megapolis of such gigantic proportions. Instead, smaller neighbourhood dreams began to be articulated in parts and bits of the city. One such area – Gurgaon – promises to fulfil the dreams of Non-Resident Indians who are being enticed to safely come back home to a chic-urban Disneyland. Another area, Mehrauli, promises to set up potential residents as gentlemen farmers. Still a third promises the proximity of the NOIDA club and a golf course. The various cities of Delhi had been established in a historical sequence of single settlements each with a different name and location. Then during the colonial era, these dispersed settlements became rooted into two permanent Delhis – the Old and the New. Today there are more than a dozen simultaneously existing sub-Delhis with the inhabitants of one not being aware of the existence of many of the others. It would perhaps be appropriate to regard contemporary Delhi now as an epic city which has a continuous

Romi Khosla

16–18
Gurgaon located in Haryana is the latest suburb of Delhi. Here the standard of living promoted equates it to NRI standards. Flats are available for the rising tide of young professionals.

narrative that ceaselessly adjusts to the rapidly changing demands of the middle class. Although surrounded by flyovers, with regulated traffic and a few metro stations, Lutyens' New Delhi is primarily a city of parks and planted avenues, where the crowds are few and the smell in the air is that of grass and floral trees. While some areas have changed radically with skyscrapers and grand new administrative buildings in a hotchpotch of architectural styles, the imperial New Delhi is still a city with spacious bungalows on wide avenues, with open spaces that carry visible and monumental memories of its distant past. Lodi Gardens is a classic example where the well-tended tombs and mausoleums of the Lodis who ruled from 1451 to 1526, stand as mute witnesses to joggers, yoga practitioners, and tourists.

By contrast, the narrative in the suburbs and in Shahjahanabad is different. Shahjahanabad has never been able to grow to epic proportions. For it is here that the poor have lived in permanent slums since 1947. It is hemmed in by the adjacent gardened banks of the river Yamuna where the remains of our rapidly growing list of erstwhile Prime Ministers are enshrined. This wasteful memorial space which should have naturally belonged to the inhabitants of Old Delhi to expand their occupations has instead become a garden of relics. Instead of growing out in space, the Old City implodes on itself with ever-increasing lofts stuffed into its rooms, where strangers brush against one another in every shadowed lane, where we cannot park but do, and where the smell of baking biscuits is flavoured by the smell of binding glue from adjacent lofts.

1
The remains of Lal Kot built
originally by the Tomaras and now
a neglected landmark of Delhi's
ancient settlements.

Romila Thapar

Romila Thapar

Rambling through Some of the Pasts of Delhi

If the traditional account of the first settlement in Delhi is to be believed then it can be said to have begun with an unhappy augury. The *Mahabharata* tells us that when the Pandavas were given their share of territory it included the Khandava-vana, the forest that had to be cleared in order to establish the territory of Indraprastha. The clearing of the forest by Arjuna and Krishna is described in graphic detail and was nothing short of a holocaust. The forest was set on fire and the fire raged fiercely for days, burning not only the trees and plants but also all the animals and those living in the forest. The agonized cries of dying creatures tore through the space of the forest. Indra tried to quench it by pouring down rain but Arjuna deflected the rain. So fierce was the conflagration that the deities who watched it wondered if they were witnessing the *mahapralaya* – the cataclysmic end of the world.

As if to annul the effect of the conflagration the settlement of Indraprastha was built on the site and the architect was the demon, Asura Maya, a Vishvakarma among the *asura*s. (There is of course a pun on the phrase *asura maya*). Indraprastha's assembly hall was renowned for its golden pillars and gem-encrusted walls that reflected a brilliant light. The floor was so polished that it was hard to tell whether it was stone or water. Duryodhana is said to have mistaken the one for the other and felt humiliated when this mistake provoked laughter. There were ponds with flowering lotuses and groves of trees perpetually in bloom. The continuous sound of entertainers and the fragrance of sandal and aloe wood enveloped the town. So great was the munificence of the Pandavas that the ten thousand brahmans assembled to bless the settlement were each given a thousand cows. This was the conventional literary description of newly emerging urban centres and such descriptions echo those of Ayodhya and Lanka in the *Ramayana*. If the description of the conflagration as a monstrous nightmare drew on poetic licence so did the description of the assembly hall and the settlement.

The two descriptions are rhetorical but also contrapuntal. The holocaust of the burning forest creates a space where a mythical magical city is then constructed. Counterpoint is essential to the epic form and carries nostalgia, a backward glance at an imagined and possibly even fantasized past. This was brought home to me vividly when excavations from part of the mound on which the Purana Qila is built revealed the settlement of earlier times going back to the first millennium BCE. The reality was not a culture of resplendent buildings but of wattle and daub and mud-brick huts, of finely made stone implements and pottery of well-levigated clay. This gradually changed to include some objects of metal – bronze and

2
Remains at Surajkund, an earlier city of the Tomaras.

subsequently iron, to a pottery fired to a lustrous finish, to human and animal terracotta figures, to mud-brick slowly giving way to burnt brick.

The settlement remained a small and not very significant one in subsequent times. It was overshadowed by larger metropolitan cities – such as Taxila in the northwest, and those of the Ganga plain – Kaushambi (near the Ganga-Yamuna confluence) and Pataliputra (modern Patna in Bihar) and later, Mathura and Kanauj. Yet the location of Indraprastha was potentially important, poised as it was on the southern edge of the Indo-Gangetic watershed. It lay squarely at the entrance to the Gangetic plain. The northern outcrops of the Aravalli hills, so much a part of the Delhi landscape, and the Terai foothills of the Himalaya further away, were the elevations commanding the approach to the Gangetic plain. At the other end it looked to the northwest of the subcontinent across the plains of the Punjab.

This potential however, was not brought into full play until the Turks, Afghans, and Mughals settled in the area. Those who ruled prior to this located themselves in the fertile middle Ganga valley. Ruling from Pataliputra allowed the Mauryas (4th–2nd century BCE) to control the extensive river trade on the Ganga system as well as the movement of goods to the east coast of India and beyond. The later shift to Mathura and Kanauj was not a shift to a more fertile region but to one that fed into the trade going to western India, the northwest, and to the Deccan and also had access to the Ganga plain. The Indo-Greeks, Shakas, and Kushanas (2nd century BCE to 4th century CE) coming from the northwest preferred Mathura to Indraprastha probably for the same reason. Harsha in the 7th century CE moved his capital from Thanesar, just north of Delhi, to Kanauj in the western Ganga plain.

Delhi carried the name of Yoganipura for a while, associated with a centre of Jain activity and with the Tomara dynasty, although inscriptions of merchants located in and around Delhi by the 13th century tend to refer to it as Dhilli or Dhillika. The Tomaras built a fort, Lal Kot, on an Aravalli outcrop and this was extended by the Chauhans and named after Prithviraja, Qila Rai Pithora. This activity possibly stemmed from an awareness of the geo-political advantages of the watershed in relation to the northwest. It is significant that the last of the Chauhans fought the Ghuri army on the watershed at Tarain.

The location of Delhi comes into its own with the establishment of the Sultanate and never looks back. The building of the Qutb Minar set within the Qila Rai Pithora is seen as

3
Ferozshah Kotla, the citadel built by the Tughluq king on the banks of the Yamuna.

4
Purana Qila – another in the series of citadels that successive rulers built in the Aravalli hills and later by the Yamuna. On the left can be seen the dome of the private mosque of Sher Shah Suri.

inaugurating the Delhi Sultanate. It has now become the logo of Delhi. One of the interesting questions seldom addressed is the extent to which there was a conscious use of the past in the buildings of the then present. Was the Qutb merely a tower of victory as it is often described, or does it carry other layers of a symbolic marker? It has been argued that pillars from early times in India, and elsewhere, were symbolic of the axis mundi, though this would be inherent to any pillar-like structure. An initial argument referred to the Buddhist complex of the stupa, the monolithic pillar, and the tree. Subsequently it is also associated with some temples where it carries an actual or supposed banner. In the Qutb complex an iron pillar of the mid-first millennium CE is juxtaposed to the Minar. Its provenance remains controversial. The inscription is a eulogy on a king named Chandra, whose identity is not absolutely certain. What was the perception of the pillar, of its inscription which could not by then be deciphered, and its location? Were there perceived connections of which we are unaware?

The notion of a symbolic marker is also underlined by the Qutb Minar being located at the site of one of the earliest conversions of a temple into a mosque. This is explained mono-causally as an act of iconoclasm, which it certainly was. But the destruction of temples by rulers of various religions – among which Hinduism and Islam are included – was occasioned by much more than religious iconoclasm. As has been frequently stated, the temple and particularly one built from royal patronage as was the temple in the fort, was a statement of power and authority, so that when the actual power that it evoked had been toppled, the temple suffered desecration. The defeat of Prithviraja at the battle of Tarain was the prelude to the conversion of the temple in the Qila Rai Pithora. This was paralleled for example in the destruction of some Chaulukya temples in western India by the Paramaras at the end of the 12th century CE. The large, royal temples that were desecrated were also treasuries of wealth collected through the offerings of donors and pilgrims and this made them susceptible to looting, as demonstrated by some kings of Kashmir in pre-Islamic times who forcibly took away the wealth of temples in times of fiscal crises.

Perhaps the Minar was to the populace more a symbol of political victory rather than the imprint of a new religion, although the accompanying mosque was stating the latter. The former is suggested by the inscriptions engraved on the Minar by masons, who repaired it each time it was struck by lightning in Khalji and Tughluq times. Significantly the repair of the

Minar is associated on each occasion with the ruler, thus Shri Sultrana Alavadi (Alauddin Khalji) and Pheroj Shahi (Firuzshah Tughluq), and it is referred to merely as a *minar* or a *jaya stambha* (pillar of victory). The dates are not given in the Hijri era but in the Samvat era, which continues from the past. The masons invoke their deity, Vishvakarma, an invocation that is reminiscent of the Asura Maya. Some record the names of the masons as Nana, Salha, Lola, and Lakshmana. A couple of them are mentioned again in a later inscription suggesting that they might have been employed regularly by the builders who maintained the Minar. With so much continuous building in the vicinity, masons and artisans probably did not face too much unemployment. The inscriptions also provide a few technical details about the repairs. As has often been said, the use of hereditary masons would have continued a tradition of workmanship from the past. But the structures they were now working on were sometimes different from those crafted by their forefathers. What would the builders have thought of these new forms?

There is yet another reason for building mosques at temple sites. In some cases this may relate to the appropriation of a pre-existing sacred space. This again has an antiquity in India, with Buddhist stupas built at megalithic burial sites, where the appropriation of sacred space is also at one level a continuity of context in that both venerate relics; or else the later conversion of some Buddhist chaityas and icons to Vaishnava and Shaiva worship. The mosque at the Qutb may well carry some trace of this notion of appropriation, given that the cloisters retained as part of the mosque carry the sculptural representation of human figures, a decorative feature disallowed by orthodox Islam.

Such an appropriation would point us in a direction that is often overlooked. Since there are no extensive remains of religious monuments in Delhi from the pre-Sultanate period, and our concerns have been focused on political history, there is a tendency to overlook the role of Delhi as a major religious and commercial centre in Islamic times: a role that is frequently tied together. Scattered among the forts and citadels inhabited by the aristocracy are the many dargahs associated with the tombs of pirs and the khanqahs of Sufi orders. If one thinks for a moment of the complex at Nizamuddin it gives substance to myriad floating thoughts born out of religious belief and sentiment and their inter-leaving with the lives of the court circles, the local populace, and visiting merchants.

5
The walls of Purana Qila in the background provide a recreational setting for a lake in its moat. On the left, one of the two surviving grand entrances to the fortress.

Sufi khanqahs covered a span of activities. There were debates with Islamic orthodoxy; there were assertions of an alternate power centre distinct from the court of the Sultan, assertions that required a distancing from the court and could end up with the Sultan cultivating the members of the khanqah who might otherwise have become political dissidents. The centres of Sufi worship were accessible to the courtiers, the townspeople, to the populace at large. Their power lay in this accessibility. Here again the form taken by the Sufi tradition echoes that of a number of earlier religious movements such as the Buddhist and Jain monks, the wandering jogis, and those who preached the centrality of bhakti. These built their strength on a flexibility of ritual and belief, with a considerable crossing of the borders between formal religions, and on a distancing from or even renunciation of, conventional authority and orthodoxy. The continuities from the past are unmistakable in some Sufi sects, which explains in part their resonance with the larger population, cutting across formal religious identities. This gave them a moral authority that could not be disregarded, neither by orthodoxy nor by political power. Hence the attempts, some of which were successful, of wooing such groups and inducting them into the centres of political and economic power or associating them with orthodoxy.

The dargahs and the khanqahs were initially located at some physical distance from the court. But they tended to get engulfed by each shift in the location of the court at Delhi, shifts that were caused by a change of dynasty. The physical locations moved from being close to the Aravalli outcrops to moving towards the river – from Qila Rai Pithora to Siri, Tughluqabad, and Jahanpanah, and to Kotla, Purana Qila, and Shahjahanabad closer to the bank of the river. The location of the capital in Mughal times sometimes alternated between Delhi and Agra. The recognition of the past becomes evident in the installation of an Ashokan

7
The tomb of Ghiyasuddin Tughluq in the citadel which was an appendage to the fortress of Tughluqabad.

column at the highest point of Firuzshah's citadel in Delhi. It was transported from Topra (in UP) on a 42-wheeled carriage to the river and then by barge down the river to Delhi, all with special care and much labour. Another Ashokan pillar was brought from Meerut (also in UP) and erected on the Delhi Ridge – an outcrop of the Aravallis. The inscriptions could not be read by now as the script had evolved and changed. But obviously there was search for legitimacy from the past and a connection sought with this past.

The repeated location of Delhi as the capital is striking. The Qutb Minar signifying the initial capital of the Sultanate, was incidentally built at Delhi and not in the city associated with the defeated Chauhan power, Ajmer. Perhaps this had to do with the proximity to the northwest and Punjab, the link areas to the homeland and crucial to Sultanate power to begin with. It was also more directly on the route carrying the trade from the northwest to the western Ganga plain. Once the location became the capital it remained so. As a capital it evoked the continuity of political power; it had an administrative structure which doubtless gradually became in-built; there were craftsmen at hand for the construction of palaces, mosques, and mausoleums who became increasingly adept at new styles of architecture; and there were the markets and merchants providing a necessary commercial base to the capital. The British, after the Revolt of 1857 also laid claim to political legitimacy by eventually shifting the capital to Delhi.

These capitals with their shifting locations, each built in the vicinity of the earlier one, were enclosed by walls and fortifications and this was yet another tradition going back to the cityscape of earlier times. (Shifting locations of capitals might be ancestral to the obsession with the "colonies" of today's Delhi, as self-sufficient settlements, obstructing the emergence of Delhi as a metropolitan city.) But when the defence of the city collapsed through major acts

Romila Thapar

of plunder from hit-and-run invaders, neighbouring populations from the countryside joined in the looting. Such arsonists were sometimes led by local landowners, of whom the richer and more powerful had their own scores to settle with a range of city people. These were occasions when the foundational conflagration was repeated with Timur Lane in 1398, Nadir Shah in 1739, Ahmed Shah Abdali in 1757, and in the quelling of the Revolt of 1857 by the British. These were in effect attacks on the polity and economy of the Sultans of Delhi and the Mughal rulers and was spurred on by the opulence of the city. The counterpoint of destruction and creation, after the initial holocaust, has hovered over the site of Delhi for many subsequent centuries.

The aristocracy suffered far less from these raids than did the townspeople. The spiriting away of the peacock throne or the Kohinoor was a disaster, but the more heart-rending damage was suffered by those who worked in the city. The disruptions brought work to a close for artisans and labourers. Markets were abandoned and trade came to a standstill. Seeking shelter in their courtyard houses, merchants waited anxiously for the departure of the marauders, particularly if their houses were also storing their more exotic merchandise. Merchants are frequently made resilient by their profession, and plundering raids punctuated the flow of trade but did not terminate it. Delhi exploited its location and after each raid resumed making its profits. In later times, even when the power of the then ruler declined or when it changed hands, other trading groups moved in such as Khatris and Jains. Protecting the profits of trade would also have required fortified capitals.

The 16th century saw the construction of the Purana Qila which encircled the only impressive mound on the river. It was of course not a natural mound, but had been built up in the earlier centuries through settlements at the same site. Did those who planned and built the fort realize that it was a settlement mound? Even if they did they seemed to have lacked much curiosity, although the presence of historians and archaeologists does not guarantee the probing of a mound. A weakness in curiosity was also displayed in recent times. When a

8 & 9
The Qutb Minar as a symbol of victory whose inscriptions informed the populace of its symbolical role.

Romila Thapar

10 *opposite*
Entrance to the tomb of Iltutmish
(circa 1235) in the Qutb complex.

partial slope of the mound was excavated and the settlements that had gone into the making of early Delhi began to be revealed, the excavation was terminated. This was done despite the fact that it was in many ways an ideal location, the slope allowing the various levels of different periods to be retained and the site being enclosed by the walls of the fort. The completion of the excavation and a possible site museum together with the structures of Sultanate and Mughal times, would have provided the rare evidence of the history of the city to the present. It was said that there was a shortage of funds and therefore the excavation could not be continued.

The building of New Delhi was a deliberate attempt at invoking history, among other things. The choice of the site was a continuation of the earlier idea of each dynasty building anew the core of its capital at the site. This underlined the status of the dynasty. In the case of colonial Delhi it was also seen as signalling the termination of Mughal rule with the British inheriting the legacy of the Mughal empire. Whereas the architecture of the Sultanate and the Mughals sought some historical links with Central Asia and incorporated features of that local tradition, colonial Delhi in its monumental buildings, was cooked from a recipe using diverse styles from Islamic and Rajput architecture with touches of European forms. A coherent style was lacking although the imperial stance was evident. The mosaic of potted rituals and forms that went into inventing the Darbar of 1911, as has been pointed out, had its counterpart in the monumental buildings of colonial Delhi. There was a deliberate recall of historical forms but their juxtaposition was arbitrary and often out of context.

The recall of history was insistent in other ways, as for example, even in something as simple as the naming of roads in New Delhi. The last of the pre-British cities, Shahjahanabad had names that described the street such as Chandni Chowk, or referred to localities and occupations. New Delhi roads were a roll-call of selected historical personalities. This was an arid way of invoking a particular kind of imperial history, and was doubtless meant to suggest that the colonial power controlled the past of India within the grid of the layout of New Delhi.

Post-colonial Delhi is revoking the British insistence on how colonial agencies defined history, by ignoring history or presenting it in ways that arouse neither curiosity nor enthusiasm. Historical monuments that are not of primary importance, are used for unlikely purposes – as stables to house animals, as space for bicycle repair shops, as dormitories for the homeless. This use is irrespective of what the original function of the structure may have been. Yet small segments of the past, such as obscure historical buildings, can be imaginatively woven into new building projects if there is sensitivity to retaining something of the past and to creating an awareness about it. Even the protection and preservation of major monuments is not a matter of priority. Those that attract tourists receive attention, the rest are subject to general unconcern. Neither the Delhi Development Authority nor the Archaeological Survey of India are interested in implementing a programme of "salvage archaeology" which could go a long way towards preventing the wiping out of that past which can still be preserved. One almost wishes for the return of a Firuzshah Tughluq who instinctively protected and conserved for us as the inheritors of Indian history, one of the finest artefactual documents from the past – the pillar of Ashoka, inscribed with his Pillar Edicts.

This is not to suggest that everything from the past must be preserved – be it buildings or culture-ways. But it is to suggest that those who live in Delhi should feel the vibrancy of the city in the interface of the past with the present. To abort the past of this city as we are now doing, is to desolate our lives as its citizens. Allowing the visibility of the past to disappear in a city space is a form of reverse conflagration – it reduces the past to ashes. And will we then be able to conjure up an Asura Maya to create even the fantasy of a magical city?

Akhilesh Mithal

The Delhi that Once Was

Time was when there existed a "Dillee";
a city marked for its excellence
in the whole wide world....

Mir Taqi "Mir", the 18th-century master of Urdu poetry,[1] composed a verse bemoaning the fate of his beloved city repeatedly subjected to invasion, massacre, arson, and despoliation. Dillee was learning the lesson that being "a heaven upon earth" is a risky business. "Mir" ascribed the calamity as arising out of the envy of the heavens. He was fleeing Dillee and his outlandish appearance aroused curiosity. His response:

Kyaa boodoabaash poochhoa hoa Poorub kay saakinoan
Hum koa ghareeb jaan kay; huns huns pukaar kay
Dillee joa eik shahar thhaa
Aalum meiyn intekhaab
Rehtey jahaan thhay muntakhib hee roazgaar kay
Uskoa fuluk ney loot kay veeraan kur diyaa
Hum rehney waaley heiyn
Usee ujaday diyaar kay

O Easterners
You judge me vagrant, vagabond and tramp
because my clothes are threadbare and my countenance melancholy
and question me, in derision, about my origin and habitat.
Know then that Dillee,
which used to be a special and chosen place
amongst the cities of the world,
attracted as its inhabitants the select and topmost members
of each profession, avocation and calling.
The city grew in eminence
until the Heavens themselves envied it.
Fate visited it with devastation.
I too once inhabited the place which is now a desolation.

The court of Mughal Emperor Shah
Alam II (1759–1806), Delhi,
circa 1800–10. Paper; 24 x 21 cm.
Photograph courtesy National
Museum, New Delhi, Acc. No. 76.559.

"Mir" also says

Dillee kay na thhay koochay
Awraaqay musawwir thhay
Joa shukl nuzur aayee
Tusweer nuzur aayee

The streets, lanes, and by-lanes of Dillee
were not mere thoroughfares, roads, passages, and alleyways:
they were gilded folios of an illuminated manuscript
where every face was a masterwork.

And again

Huft iqleem hur galee heiyn kuheen
Dillee sey bhee diyaar hoatey heiyn

Is there another place where you can experience
all seven climes of the world
in each alley, passage, and thoroughfare?
How then is it possible for any city to equal Dillee?

2
The Diwaan-i-Khaas-o-Aam in the
Red Fort for public audiences built
in red sandstone. The inner palaces
along the river were clad in marble.

Akhilesh Mithal

3
The Shah Burj in the Red Fort is one of the marble pavilions aligned along the river front with the other imperial chambers. Only the king and his children had the use of this pavilion.

The layout and buildings of Shahjahan's Dillee with the palace fort La'al Qilaa (Red Fort) as its heart and the Ja'ama Masjid as its sanctum formed the noblest assemblage of masses, spaces, water, and greenery in the world of the 17th century. The design succeeded in bringing together solid stone and mortar buildings with flowing and still water interspersed with lush and ordered vegetation to make for a veritable paradise upon earth.

Shahjahanabad which evoked the poignant verse of "Mir", was not the first Dillee to rival heaven on earth. This distinction belongs to Indraprastha (1500 BCE).

The legendary Indraprastha came into being as the Pandavas' capital. In dividing the empire Dhritarashtra gave the capital Hastinapura on the banks of the Ganga to his sons, the Kauravas, while Khandavaprastha on the banks of the Yamuna was apportioned to his nephews, the Pandavas. While no traces are left of the city, the epic in which its creation is recounted – the *Mahabharata* – continues to be part of a living tradition and the hyperbolic description of the Pandava capital (see preceding essay by Thapar) remains an article of faith with Indians. This was the verbal model that was used by B.R. Chopra to build the sets of the hit TV series of the 1980s on the epic. Vyasa's verse makes the long-vanished golden halls come alive and recreates the beauty and grace of the city built to rival paradise on earth:

> Then, girded by a moat wide as the sea and protected by a wall reaching high up to the heavens and white as the fleecy clouds or the beams of the full moon, that foremost of cities looked as if it was the capital of the asuras who rule the regions below the earth. It stood adorned with palatial mansions and numerous gates...looking like clouds and high as mountains, stocked with weapons to dispel attackers. The gates were so well wrought that they would not suffer even a small dent from the weapons of the attackers.

Their surfaces bristled with sharp projecting darts to prevent war elephants and battering rams from causing them damage....

Inside the city the streets were wide and so well laid out that there was little fear of accidents.

In a delightful and auspicious part of the city rose the palace of the Pandavas filled with every kind of treasure and jewels making it look like the abode of Kubera, God of Wealth.

When the city was built brahmans well acquainted with the Vedas and conversant with every language came to dwell in it. Many, many merchants also moved in.

Although the paradise is now lost and no artefact has been uncovered by the spade of the archaeologist, the name Indraprastha survives to be invoked in Hindu prayers offered at birth, marriage, *griha pravesh* (entering a new dwelling), and death.

Dillee was conquered by Qutbuddin Aiybek, army chief of the Ghorid Sultan Shihabuddin Muhammad aka Muizuddin in 1192. In the 13th and 14th centuries the Dillee dream took the shape of citadels and walled cities to protect inhabitants from the dreaded Mongols who had conquered Lahore in 1241, and made repeated attacks on India up to 1329.[2] Sonorous sobriquets and grand titles such as *Qubbat-ul-Islam* "the refuge of Islam" and "a twin of paradise" were bestowed upon it. The coins of the period struck in the city mint give the city an honorific Hazrat Dillee. Amir Khusro (1235–1310) used both these terms and also equated the city with heaven.

As Mongol hordes were invading India, in 1303 Alauddin Khilji built the fortified city of Siri known as the second Dillee. In 1320 Sultan Ghiyasuddin (aka Ghaziuddin) Tughluq built Tughluqabad with its massive cyclopean walls. Fakhruddin Muhammad Jauna Shah aka Muhammad bin Tughluq (1325–51) provided for Mongol incursions and built fortifications to

4
Jama Masjid, Shahjahan's congregational mosque, is the largest in India and dominates the city and views from the Red Fort.

encompass both Siri and Tughluqabad within protective walls and called it *Jahanpanah* or "refuge of the world" in 1327. This saved the city from Tarmashirin's raid in 1329 although Meerut was invested and conquered and the Doab (area watered by the Ganga and Yamuna) plundered and devastated.

Mongol pressure contributed in a more positive fashion to Delhi's primacy. The city fast became a refuge for those in Khurasan and Central Asia – whether bureaucrats, soldiers, scholars, or mystics – who fled from Mongol terror.

According to the 14th-century traveller Ibn Batuta, Dillee had a vast area and population. The Egyptian encyclopedist al-Umari (d. 1349) credits the city with a circumference of forty miles. He was told that it contained seventy hospitals and a thousand seats of learning (madrasas).

The continuous building programme does not support the theory that Dillee was abandoned for Daulatabad Deogir.

What actually happened around 1327 was that the principal Muslim residents of the old city together with their dependants and considerable households were dispatched south. The exception was military personnel. The contemporary historian Ziyauddin Barani states clearly that "the amirs, maliks and troops" remained with the Sultan in the north when their families were in Daulatabad Deogir. Isami's (circa 1350) bitter reference to the city being repopulated with Hindus most likely refers to the drafting of peasants for the proposed incursion into Khurasan. The recruitment of the Khurasan force had to coincide with the migration to Daulatabad in order to minimize food consumption in Dillee and setting of impossible targets for grain producers. Barani records that the Khurasan force had to be disbanded just a year after raising as there were insufficient funds to pay salaries.

Mostly tombs and monuments remain from the Sultanate period, and the paradisial cities have become the dust of history.

The next attempt to create a Paradise upon earth was in 1639.

In his 12th regnal year Shahjahan renamed Agra "Akbarabad" to honour his grandfather, Jalaluddin Muhammad Akbar, and embarked on the project of building a new Dillee to be called Shahjahanabad.

5
Jama Masjid inscription.

6
The Diwan-i-Khaas or Private Audience Hall in the Red Fort was adjacent to Shahjahan's private quarters. These marble-clad structures had allusions to paradise.

7

The Scales of Justice in the Red Fort of Shahjahanabad in gilded relief within a carved marble screen. Below flows the Canal of Paradise coming from the Shah Burj lotus pool.

Shahjahan was tenth in direct line from Amir Timur (the Tamerlane of European legend) who after conquering Dillee in 1398/1399 took 22,000 Indian masons, stonecutters, and craftsmen with him to build his dream city, Samarkand, in what is now Uzbekistan. Shahjahan, following Timur, wanted to leave the impress of his reign upon the world by creating the marvellous in each of his areas of interest. Monuments, thrones, musical modes, jewels, cities, waterworks, and the halls witnessing the administration of justice all gained from this enthusiasm.

Shahjahan started his career as builder by redesigning the pavilions of the Kabul gardens during his father Jahangir's reign. By the time he took up the Shahjahanabad project he had proved his mettle by the marvels he had created such as the mausoleum of his wife (the Taj Mahal) and the Peacock Throne wrought for ceremonial use in court.

Shahjahan had extraordinary talent in military as well as civil areas. He had mastered the appraisal and evaluation of gems, jewels, calligraphy, and painting besides honing his genius in architecture. Perhaps the architectonic qualities of balance and harmony approached perfection in his case because of Shahjahan's passionate cultivation of classical Indian music. His anthology of a thousand dhrupads (a classical musical mode) can be seen in the National Museum in Delhi. As a seal of approval he lent his own name to each composition.

Shahjahan's reign witnessed a phenomenal growth of wealth in India because the wise and enlightened policies of Akbar (a low assessment of revenue and strictness in collection) were continued along with extension of irrigation and agriculture into hitherto undeveloped areas. City bazaars grew while the expansion of the empire made the area of trade larger. This wealth combined with the personality of the Emperor gave material shape to ideas and designs excelling any that had been executed in earlier times. Building activity reached an unprecedented scale and provided jobs for skilled and unskilled labour, while money which

Akhilesh Mithal

had lain idle in treasuries came out into circulation. Shahjahanabad instantly and at birth became the cynosure of the world and lived up to the claim of being "a Paradise on Earth". Its palace citadel (the Red Fort) covered 105 acres walled with red sandstone of a uniform quality and colour. The crystal clear water of a twenty-acre moat encircled the huge structure in a liquid ring to give the whole a softness and delicacy. The green and red of the gulabi (rose) garden outside the walls added a verdancy to the appearance of the palace fort. The pavilions and palaces within the red sandstone walls were white marble inlaid with semi-precious stones and topped with domes of gold. The roof of the Diwaan-i-Khaas was solid silver plated with gold and encrusted with jewels. The Peacock Throne fashioned out of 1,250 kilograms of pure gold and encrusted with jewels worth fifty lakh rupees in 1631, stood in the projecting elevation called the emperor's balcony (Nasheymun-i-Zilley Ilaahee) of the assembly of peers and commoners (Diwaan-i-Khaas-o-Aam).

The area between the stone structures of the Diwaan-i-Khaas-o-Aam and the Naqqaarkhaana (ceremonial drum house) was covered by a brocade and cloth of gold canopy woven in Ahmadabad and called Dal Baadal (group of clouds). This unique and glorious textile was supported by silver pillars covered with gold plate and encrusted with jewels. A silver railing and a gold railing in the Diwaan-i-Khaas-o-Aam separated nobles according to the rank held. Music was played throughout the time the court was in session.

The main function of the court whether held in the Diwaan-i-Khaas-o-Aam or the Diwaan-i-Khaas (for the assembly of peers and other chosen notables) was the administration of justice. Justice in the application and interpretation of laws; justice in rewards and appointments, promotions and transfers, postings and dismissals, was delivered in full public view in these courts. The function of the architecture and the embellishments and ornamentation was to provide an appropriate setting and create the aura of magnificence and splendour befitting the majesty of Justice. Opulence was not an end in itself and functioned as a background against which justice was done and "seen to be done" in full public view.

The Emperor, Zilley Ilaahee "Shadow of God Upon Earth", could be seen and heard from any point in the area of the Diwaan-i-Khaas-o-Aam with none of the columns and pillars impeding or obscuring the view. The attempt at recreating paradise was clear and unambiguous.

8
The Naqqaar Khaana or Drum Room is located across a courtyard opposite the Hall of Public Audience. From here the drummers announced the royal presence.

Paradise has flowing water. The palace fort, the streets, byways, alleys, mansions, mosques, seminaries, hospitals, colleges, and baths (hamaams), had each its own water dimension. Canals, pools, tanks, fountains, and waterfalls helped water the city and keep it cool in a gracious manner.

Of all the waterways the pride of Shahjahan was the canal that fell in a rippling cascade down the marble chute in the Shahburj pavilion. Flowing along the terrace bordering the Hayat Bakhsh garden it traversed the stately edifices lining the eastern wall of the palace, the hamaams, the Diwaan-i-Khaas, and the Khwaabgaah. Silently gliding below the Scales of Justice (Mizaan-i-'Adl) it crossed a sunbathed court into the Rang Mahal. Thence, still flowing south, it passed through the Little Rang Mahal or Mumtaz Mahal and other pavilions sending out shoots to feed many channels and streams.

Niccolao Manucci, who travelled in India in the second half of the 17th century records: Shahjahan ordered some beautiful fish thrown into the canal with gold rings in their fins, each ring having one ruby and two seed pearls.

Akhilesh Mithal

Francois Bernier in his *Travels in the Mughal Empire A.D. 1656–1668* says:

> Nearly every chamber has its reservoir or running water at the door; on every side there are gardens, delightful alleys, shady retreats, streams, fountains, grottos, deep excavations that afford shelter from the sun by day, lofty divans and terraces on which to sleep cool at night.

The canal was called "Waterway of Paradise", Neharey Bahisht and the Court of Special Audience (Diwaan-i-Khaas) had the verse:

> *Agar firdaus bur rouey zameenast, hameenastoa hameenastoa hameenast*

> If there is Paradise anywhere upon Earth, It is here! It is here! It is here!

written in letters of gold on its wall.

The canal connects the public area of the Diwaan-i-Khaas with the private apartments of the emperor (Khwaabgaah or rest area; Tasbeehkhaana or sanctuary for prayers and for telling a rosary).

A thick screen sculpted out of flawless, white and translucent, jewel-quality marble divided the public areas such as the Diwaan-i-Khaas from the private apartments. Water flowed beneath the screen while its top carried the Scales of Justice.

The Scales of Justice are seen floating in ether amidst astral bodies to illustrate the position of the stars in the horoscope of Shahjahan and provide legitimacy to the title Sahib Qiran (Lord of the Auspicious Conjunction of Venus and Jupiter) and justify the wielding of the power of Life and Death.

This emblem of the Mughal dynasty was honoured by the emperors and earned the title "Great or Grande Mughal" for the first six of them.

Zilley Ilaahee was the address used for the Emperor; he was on earth what God was in the Heavens. Justification was needed for such an absolute power to be acceptable. This was provided by the administration of justice. He therefore lived with its sculpted representation whether he was at work or resting and relaxing. The water flowing below the scales was placed to give a sense of rest, ease, and tranquillity.

During the period the city was being built, 1639–48, Shahjahan inspected the works in progress and improved the design with timely and informed interventions. The completion of the project saw him ride into the city on a gold howdah atop a majestic tusker. He showered largesse scattered in the shape of miniature coins of gold and silver (*nissar*) while his eldest son Dara Shikoh who stood behind him scattered enamelled jewels fashioned to look like almonds, pistachios, and other fruit.

After completing the palace fort project and seeing the palaces and gardens of the princes and princesses coming up inside and outside the walled city area, the emperor took up the project of building the congregational mosque, Ja'ama Masjid: Masjid-i-Jahaan Numaa. This was the largest congregational mosque in the world for many centuries.

12
The Jama Masjid and Shahjahanabad seen from one of the minarets.

Standing in the eastern verandah of the mosque and looking towards the palace fort has an electric effect on the visitor who can see the buildings relate to each other as parts of the same organic whole conceived and executed by a genius who "built like a giant and finished his works like a jeweller".

There are five inscriptions on the building praising the structure and an equal number, its builder. The white speckles in the veins of the red sandstone were likened to trapped and enmeshed glow-worms by the chronicler of Shahjahan's reign. The lotus appears in various forms and shapes and the walls are decorated with garlands of flowers and leaves in the style of *bandanwaar*s which traditionally decorate temples and the venue of marriages and worship to provide colour and perfume to Indian celebrations.

The dream of Dillee as Paradise may have come to Shahjahan from the Indraprastha of the Pandavas. The *Mahabharata*, translated into Persian in the reign of Akbar as the *Razmnaameh*, achieved immediate popularity with the nobles from Central Asia and Persia. Mirza Abdul Rahim Khaneykhaanaan ("general of generals") took permission to have a copy made for his personal library.

Shahjahanabad enjoyed great power and riches from its birth right up to the battle of Karnal on February 13, 1739. The comment of the victor, Nadir Shah: "Indians know how to die in battle but, and alas! not how to fight and win" showed that the Indians had failed to keep abreast of developments in the tactics of war. Seven hundred camel- and elephant-loads of jewels along with the Kohinoor, and gold vessels and furniture wrought out of bullion including the Peacock Throne, formed the booty taken from Dillee and Agra by Nadir Shah. The weakness of the Mughal was exposed and the looting which started with Nadir Shah continued for centuries thereafter.

Shahjahanabad repeatedly suffered the indignity of pillage, arson, and vandalism from 1739 to 1947. The water features such as the Neharey Bahisht canal which irrigated the gardens and watered the city, the ordinary wells and the step wells (baaolees), lakes, ponds, fountains, and gardens have disappeared along with the trees lining its broad avenues and crowding its gardens. The river has become a sewer and been forced away from its walls and monuments.

Shahjahan's Dillee, a Paradise upon Earth is today reduced to the status of a slum. This is truly the tale of a Paradise Lost.

The British New Delhi is an attempt at an imperial essay by lesser mortals. The structures lack grandeur and majesty because the concerns of the builders were petty. The proportions of the Viceregal Lodge were set not to create a presence to proclaim the grandeur of the British Empire but to make sure that it rose to a level slightly higher than the pinnacle of the Ja'ama Masjid of Shahjahan. The traders of a poor country turned conquerors could not possibly rival a prince of the House of Timur.

What has come after the departure of the British is worse. There is no central idea or theme and no question of a dream. There is a Meccano building on Janpath and a Pyjama building in Siri.

The dream has truly died, and an ugly reality has taken over.

NOTES

1. Mir Taqi Mir was sixteen or seventeen years old in 1739, the year of Nadir Shah's invasion of Delhi and 87 or 88 years old when he died in 1810. "Mir", a great master of Urdu poetry is acknowledged as such by subsequent greats such as Asadulla Khan "Ghalib" (d. 1866) and Raghupati Sahay "Firaq" (d. 1984). Mir's poetry is world class with the verses dealing with love rarely equalled and never surpassed.

2. The Mongols first attacked India in 1241 when they invaded and conquered Lahore. Their subsequent attacks were in 1245–46, 1257–58, 1285, 1287, 1292, 1297– 98, 1299–1300, 1303, 1305, 1306, 1322, and 1329.

1

The east front of the Viceroy's Palace.
The last of the royal palaces of the
Empire, it was also the largest one
ever built by the British.

Romi Khosla

Glory of Empire: Imperial Delhi

The transfer of the British Indian capital from Calcutta to Delhi was announced by King-Emperor George V at his Durbar in Delhi in 1911 during the first and only visit of a British monarch to the country they believed to be the "jewel in the crown". Calcutta had served as the nerve centre of the East India Company since 1774 when Warren Hastings (1774–85) had become Governor General. But, under the Company, the focus of imperial activities was concentrated at the ports and the effective writ of Hastings was intended to control the ports and hinterland of Calcutta, Bombay, and Madras. However, the rebellion of 1857 changed that strategy since the British believed that the crumbling inland court of the Mughal Emperor Bahadur Shah Zafar in Delhi had made a desperate bid to restore its power and had provided the inspiration and facilities for the conspiracy that had incited the troops to rebel. The memory of a splendid Mughal empire centred in the Red Fort in Delhi therefore had to be replaced in the minds of the Indians with the far greater glory of the British empire. Put in terms of heritage, the extraordinary Mughal architectural achievements of Shahjahanabad had to be outdone by an even grander imperial architectural heritage. In the words of Lord Stamfordham, the Principal Private Secretary to King George: "We must now let him (the native Indian) see for the first time the power of western science and art and civilisation" (*Indian Summer*, p. 73).

The energetic construction activities of the Mughal emperors in Lahore, Agra, and Delhi had left behind an unusual architectural heritage that was not only vast in scale but also unique in its grandeur and beauty. The monuments and urban institutions that the Mughal emperors sponsored and funded including Humayun's Tomb in Delhi, the Taj Mahal in Agra, the Forts in Lahore, Agra, and Delhi, Jama Masjid and indeed the whole of Shahjahanabad and Fatehpur Sikri had brought to Indian architectural history a uniqueness of style and cultural fusion that was truly extraordinary. By the time Shahjahan was forced to conclude his building spree, the Mughal treasury had already been depleted of the earlier surpluses carefully collected during the good times of conquests and trade. Within a few decades, his successors had been reduced to destitute monarchs with an army of retainers who had nowhere else to go and no means to survive except to linger about the citadel and wait for the meagre handouts given by the court officials. Thus it was that a century and a half after Shahjahan died, British soldiers marched their cavalcade down Chandni Chowk, led by General Gerald Lake who summarily took control of the administration of Delhi and formally declared the end of the Mughal empire. Henceforth, the occupant of the throne in the Delhi citadel was to be known simply as the King of Delhi. As Shahjahanabad continued its steep decline into a dense slum condition, it was once more time for yet another Delhi to be founded. So it was that just over a century after General Lake marched down Chandni Chowk, Lord Hardinge of Penhurst arrived in India as the new Governor General and guided the events which concluded with King George's announcement that Delhi was to become the capital of the empire in the subcontinent.

The intention to move the capital to Delhi meant that the offices of the Viceroy, Commander-in-Chief, the Government of India, the Legislative Assembly, and a host of officials would have to move to the new city. The commercial community in Calcutta deeply resented this announcement. But, as Lord Hardinge explains in *My Indian Years*:

> Before I arrived in India, I was well aware that the province of Bengal was seething with sedition, the outcome of the policy of partition [of Bengal done by Lord Curzon]. Dacoits and assassinations of police and informers were almost a daily occurrence in Calcutta and its neighbourhood, and it was practically impossible to secure a conviction by the ordinary process of law.

The partitioning of Bengal had continued to cause enormous difficulties for the British administration in Calcutta. The Durbar of 1911, at which King George was present, therefore presented a unique opportunity to announce that Calcutta was no longer convenient as the centre of power. Clearly it was a declaration to the Bengalis that since they had not mended their ways and had continued to "seethe" they could do so within a lesser provincial territory rather than a national one. Behind the scenes, within the confidential corridors of the administration, there had already been preparatory work done to effect this change of capital. The British had not been happy with Calcutta as capital after 1858. Lord Curzon had considered moving the capital to Agra. Later, Lord Lawrence had mooted the idea of shifting

2

The ceremonial approach to the palace is dominated by the base of the Jaipur Column in the centre of the forecourt. It was gifted by Sir Sawai Madho Singh, Maharaja of Jaipur, in celebration of the founding of New Delhi.

the capital to Delhi, but the Council was opposed to it. Finally it was Lord Hardinge who determined that the British should push ahead with the move and use the opportunity of the 1911 Durbar to launch the initiative amongst the Indians by making a formal announcement. He was strongly supported by Sir John Jenkins, the Home Member of the Council, who wrote to Lord Hardinge in June 1911 that there was need of "a bold stroke of statesmanship which would give universal satisfaction and mark a new era in the history of India". Jenkins believed that the Durbar announcement would initiate a "change that would be magical since, in the imagination of the masses of the people, Delhi and Empire have been associated from time immemorial". Lord Hardinge was an astute administrator. He realized that he would need to link the moving of the capital to a larger administrative shuffle. He drafted a secret memorandum and circulated it to his Council members asking them to approve of four administrative changes:

1. Move the capital from Calcutta to Delhi.
2. Create a United Bengal and change its status to that of a Presidency.
3. Create a new Lieutenant Governorship for Bihar and Orissa with Patna as its capital.
4. Restore the charge of Assam under a Chief Commissioner.

The Secretary of State in London gave full approval to the four proposed changes but directed that the announcements of the Unification of Bengal and the move to Delhi be kept absolutely secret till the King formally made the announcement. This need for secrecy assumed paramount importance. The Delhi Durbar camp was organized in a way that ensured this secrecy. In order to prepare and print the requisite gazettes, news sheets, and draft announcements, a secret "press camp" was established and called "mystery camp". It was surrounded by troops and police and all the announcements were sealed in envelopes to be

3
The Mughal-styled pleasure garden of the Viceroy in the rear court of the palace was looked after by more than 400 gardeners.

distributed only at the time of the official announcement. Lord Hardinge describes that moment in his memoirs of India:

> The King rose and read the statement in a clear voice which was heard distinctly by all the 4,000 principal Durbaris present. It came like a bombshell. At first there was a deep silence of profound surprise, followed in a few seconds by a wild burst of cheering. At the same time, the Government officials broke the seals of the official Gazette prepared beforehand in the "Mystery camp" and distributed them broadcast throughout the amphitheatre.

Many at the time interpreted this move as the first sign that England intended to stay in India permanently. Somehow there had always been that lingering feeling amongst many Indians that as long as Calcutta was the capital of the empire in India, there was always a possibility that the British would leave by sea as they had arrived, either of their own accord, or in the event of a revolution led from Bengal.

Events moved fast after the Durbar. During their stay in Delhi, Lord Hardinge writes:
> the King and Queen expressed to me their wish to lay the foundation stones of the new capital of India. The proposal presented considerable difficulty since it was an open question as to where the site of the new city would really be found. It proved later that the site on which they were laid was not selected for the new capital and a year afterwards I had these stones quietly removed and placed in an honoured position in the secretariat building in the new city.

The British government in London moved swiftly to support this move. A committee consisting of Captain Swinton, former member of the London County Council, Edwin Lutyens the architect, and Brodie a sanitary engineer from Liverpool were sent to India and charged with the task of selecting the site for the capital. Lord Hardinge was not too impressed with the committee members and commented that they seemed to have spent their time wandering about on an elephant without having had any success. In 1912, they initially selected a site north of Shahjahanabad, including the Metcalfe Estate, and presented their proposals to Hardinge. But his reaction to this site was hostile. He describes the event in a way that gives himself all the credit for the final selection:

> Having been informed that [The Earl of] Crewe's committee of experts had selected and approved a site and that the layout had been flagged for my inspection and criticism, I went from Simla to Delhi with a considerable staff of technical experts, including three of the best engineers. The moment I saw the selected site I realised its objections. It would be hot; it had no views; and it had no room for expansion. After consultation for more than two hours I told the assembled staff that I would rather not build a new capital at all than build it on that site.

4
Lutyens' sketch showing the greater height of the Viceroy's Palace over the Jama Masjid in Shahjahanabad. The Jaipur Column's echo of the minarets is not coincidental.

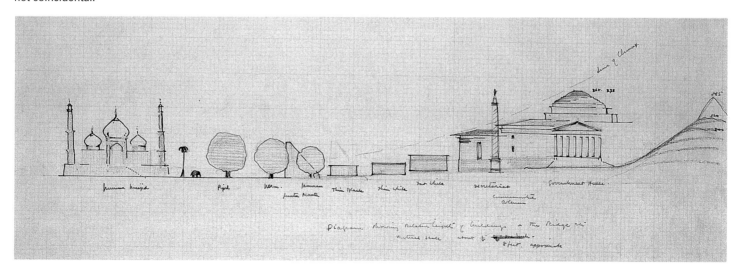

Romi Khosla

Lord Hardinge was not only a decisive administrator; he took care to be perceived as such by his subordinate staff. He continues his account of events on that day:

> I asked to be left alone for a quarter of an hour before coming to a decision, and at its close I rejected the site as impossible. I then mounted and asked Hailey [Later Sir Malcolm and then Lord Hailey, Governor of the United Provinces], Commissioner of Delhi, to accompany me to choose a new site, and we galloped over the plain to a hill some distance away. From the top of the hill there was a magnificent view embracing old Delhi and all the principal monuments situated outside the town, with the River Jumma winding its way like a streak in the foreground at a little distance. I said at once to Hailey, "This is the site for Government House", and he readily agreed. On examination I observed that the area of the top of the hill was hardly adequate for a fine Government House with all its necessary adjuncts, but one of the engineers who was present said at once that there would be no difficulty in cutting off the top of the hill so as to make a fine and broad base for building upon. The idea struck me as novel, but it was confirmed and accepted by all and the site adopted. It was equally approved by the experts [meaning the committee] from England.

5
Three urban symbols of the Imperial city placed as chess pieces in the ordered layout of the capital: the memorial canopy to house the statue of King George V, the perpetual fountains, and the All India War Memorial Arch known as India Gate.

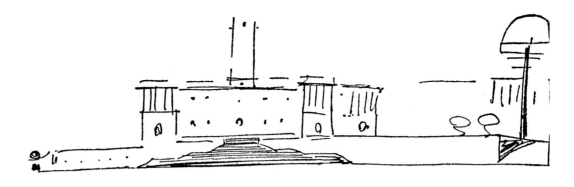

6
Lutyens' sketch showing the preferred location of the steps in the upper sketch. The lower sketch showing steps placed in the centre of the capital complex was to be avoided so that the "swarming millions" were kept away.

The Raisina Hill site so selected by Hardinge at the end of a quick gallop was to eventually be the site for the acropolis consisting of Government House (later designated as the Viceregal Lodge) and the Secretariat buildings. Although Hardinge had visualized the site being dominated solely by Government House as the crowning symbol of regal authority over the city, he did concede later, as the master planning drawings and concepts developed, to Baker's proposal for an acropolis that combined Government House with the administrative buildings as part of an architectural ensemble that would serve and be perceived more as a new citadel than the site for a stand-alone palace. The Mughal citadel of the Red Fort was a very significant architectural ensemble that had at one time not only accommodated the entire household of the Emperor, but also the entire facilities of the Mughal government. Enclosed within the fort walls, this ensemble was set around an elaborate Persian-style garden. Such a regal setting within a garden landscape had European parallels too in Versailles and other palaces in France. Thus it was that Government House too became attached to a splendid garden. It was Mughal in style because Lord and Lady Hardinge happened to visit Kashmir and "fell in love with the gardens of Srinagar". Lady Hardinge wrote to Lutyens, "I should love a Moghul garden with terraces to start from the very top of the ridge and come to the house" (*Life of Sir Edwin Lutyens*).

The 1912 sketch by Lutyens showing the dominant position of the Government House over the minarets of Jama Masjid was clearly intended to confirm the diminution of Shahjahanabad to the status of a subordinate native city (*Indian Summer*, p. 78). The effort to demonstrate the superiority of Western civilization was now in full swing and the detractors from that effort were soon sidelined. Robert Byron, a correspondent of *Country Life* wrote in 1931:

> Whilst official opinion in England and India was demanding a fusion of national motifs, Lutyens sought solutions on a less superficial basis. Whilst holding fast to the principles of humanist architecture – line, proportion, mass – he discovered from Moghul builders how these principles might be adapted to a land whose material conditions necessitate their modification.

Byron was being accommodating to Lutyens whose own thoughts and reactions were clearly revealed in his quest for greatness:

> My everlasting prayer is for the greatness and help of a Wren or Newton. If Wren had built in India, it would have been something so different to anything we know of his that we cannot name it.

For Lutyens, Wren was a model because he merged English architectural forms with Italian prototypes, while Newton symbolized reason and mathematics – cornerstones of Western civilization. It was about the time that Patrick Geddes came to India. He arrived in 1914 hoping to display the panels of an exhibition that he had prepared on a civic city. Unfortunately a German warship sank the boat carrying the panels and Geddes had to tour India without his material. He travelled from city to city, covering the subcontinent, propagating his views on the organic nature of the city. His notion of the city, influenced undoubtedly by the same Garden City movement that had influenced Lutyens, was diametrically opposed to what was being conceived for New Delhi. On the planning of sewers, for instance, Geddes wrote, "instead of the nineteenth century European city panacea – of Everything to the sewer! the right maxim for India is the traditional rural one, of Everything to the soil." (*Cities of Tomorrow*, p. 245.) Geddes believed that "city life, like organic and individual life, exists and develops with the harmonious functioning of all its organs and their adaptation to all its needs…." Lutyens could not understand Geddes. He commented, "He seems to have talked rot in an insulting way and I hear he is going to tackle me! A crank who doesn't know his subject. He talks a lot, gives himself away and then loses his temper." (*Cities of Tomorrow*, p. 247.) Geddes's approach to the city was akin to that of a biologist who regarded the city as an organism that needed careful surgery and healing in order to protect its historical tissue and its natural dynamism. Lutyens, on the other hand, saw the city as a symbol of not only colonial power, but also of a new environment that would reflect the Fabian concerns of Ebenezer Howard about the ideal place for the ideal citizen. For both Hardinge and Lutyens, the city of Shahjahanabad had nothing to offer that could be emulated or salvaged. It was a living shell with the remnants of a decayed and spent empire and its citizens were potentially rebellious and uncontrollable because they lived in narrow alleys with little daylight and bad hygienic conditions. The new city needed not only visionary planning but also strong civil engineering logic that would pipe in fresh water and carry away sewage for safe treatment.

The designers of New Delhi were a mixed team of planners and civil engineers, including the original committee members and the planner Henry Lancaster. They worked under the sharp gaze of Hardinge and his band of supportive engineers. In addition, the planners also had to hear the opinions of other influential amateurs who were well connected either to the royal family or senior government officials in London. One of them was Sir Bradford Leslie who proposed a lake by damming the Yamuna. Once the stamp of the imperial gesture on Indian soil had been finalized in the layout of the new city, the next task of appointing the architects began. Herbert Baker who had designed major buildings in Pretoria for the government of South Africa was invited to join Lutyens as the collaborating architect of the city. The work was divided between the two prima donnas with Lutyens tackling Government House and Baker the vast ensemble of the Secretariat buildings. Baker was quick to realize the importance of Raisina Hill as the key architectural setting of the city. He worked diligently to devise concepts that would enable the Secretariat complex to share the same setting as Government House. Hardinge needed to be convinced. Eventually, in the face of Baker's persuasive arguments, he made a rather hurried decision without fully realizing the implication of sacrificing his cherished idea of the exclusive setting of Government House on the crest of Raisina Hill. Baker had already drafted a note to Lutyens to obtain his approval (*Life of Sir Edwin Lutyens*):

We are of the opinion that both buildings should be raised on a common platform, so that the approach to the space between the Secretariats and that in front of the Government House should be a dignified flight of steps, with a sloping road for processions and special occasions. Our reasons are:

1. The panorama of old cities and buildings which is a convincing argument in favour of the south site should be accessible to all.
2. The old buildings that have most impressed the imagination of mankind are those raised upon an eminence, such as those of ancient Greek cities and the Capitol of Rome.
3. The raised place, denied to ordinary traffic of streets would have an air of quiet and privilege.
4. The lifting of the buildings on a platform seems to us an important characteristic of those we have seen in India. If we may find it difficult to copy the latter, we can at least follow the spirit of the buildings of the country.

Having ensured that the concerns of imperial planning were effectively in place, the field was left clear for the two architects to battle over their respective masterpieces. Lutyens could not have been happy with Baker's move to convert the stand-alone site of Government House into acropolis, but had to give way in the face of Baker's irresistible arguments. He accepted the idea of some ceremonial steps to gain access to the acropolis but wanted them located on the side. He commented:

They would come very well in themselves, axial with either block; but would this not lead away from the centre – the sun of the Lord Sahib's dome? It looks well centrifugally but I want something more centripetal, and the wider plateau may help this. But we don't want "mosque steps" here like Jami Masjid for the swarming millions to sit on – do we? But if we do, they could be where they could see the procession up the sloping via sacra.

Eventually the steps for the "swarming millions" were detached from the acropolis and were placed on either side of the central vista completely separate from the approach to the capitol complex. The issue of the approach steps was resolved by hiding the steps behind parapet walls that led them sideways to either side of the Secretariat wings. As the work proceeded, the tensions between Baker and Lutyens escalated into a full-scale fight with both

7
Connaught Place, built to rival Chandni Chowk, was intended as the premier and fashionable shopping arcade of the new capital city.

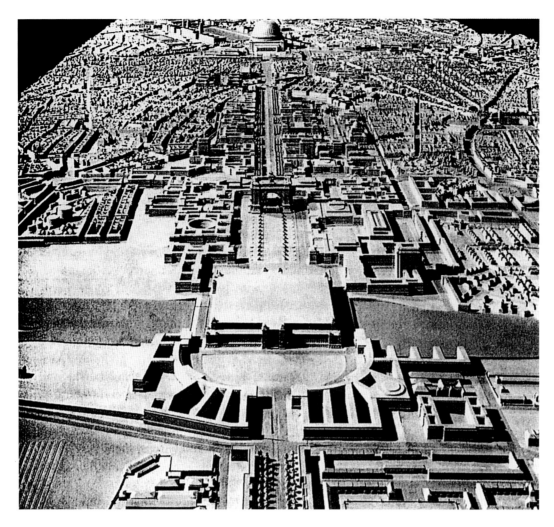

8
Not unlike Lutyens' Delhi, Speer's Berlin had a triumphal arch, an axis leading to the palace of the Third Reich. Both visions for capitals to last a thousand years.

architects often sitting together at unavoidable meetings but speaking to each other only through intermediaries. However, despite the bitterness between Baker and Lutyens, the emphasis on visualizing the new capital as a city of monuments remained the principal influence that determined the direction of avenues and the location of the key buildings.

Ironically, the unmistakable imprint of New Delhi's monumentality was to impress Hitler's architect Albert Speer whose 1931 vision of the new German identity was symbolized in the New Berlin of the Reich. The similarities between Speer's vision of Berlin and Lutyens' vision of New Delhi are remarkable. Both have a central grand avenue as the key processional axis passing through a Roman-styled gateway. Both avenues culminate at a large domed structure – the New Delhi one to house the viceroy, and the Berlin one for the absolute ruler, the fuehrer. (*Cities of Tomorrow*, p. 213). One city was intended to demonstrate the political, military, and economic power of the British empire while the other was intended to do the same for Germany. Both the Empire and the Third Reich were intended to last for a thousand years.

REFERENCES

Byron, Robert, *Country Life*, June 8, 1931.

Hall, Peter, 2001, *Cities of Tomorrow*, Oxford.

Hardinge of Penhurst, Charles Hardinge, 1948, *My Indian Years, 1910–1916: The Reminiscences of Lord Hardinge of Penhurst*, London.

Hussey, C., 1950, *The Life of Sir Edwin Lutyens*, London, New York.

Irving, Robert, 1981, *Indian Summer, Lutyens, Baker and Imperial Delhi*, Delhi, New Haven, London.

Ravinder Kaur

Claiming Community through Narratives: Punjabi Refugees in Delhi

In popular imagination, Delhi is identified as one of the Punjabi cities located outside the actual Punjab. The association is so strong that few recall Punjabis as the "original refugees", the "outsiders" who "invaded" Delhi and its culture in 1947. This amnesia is most visible among the Punjabis themselves who now lay claim to the city as much as the Kayastha Hindus[1] and the remaining Muslim populace of Old Delhi. This is not to suggest that the trauma of Partition has disappeared, but that it has stopped being a dominant presence in the everyday lives of both the "refugees" as well as the "locals". Half a century has blurred the categories of "refugees" and "residents", more so when the "refugees" have come to dominate most facets of the city from business, politics, media, to artistic and literary expressions.

Somewhere along the way the category of refugee has melted to produce citizens of post-colonial India who are more comfortable with their identity as Indians rather than ethnic Punjabis whose grand/parents escaped from internecine ethnic cleansing in West Punjab. The distant ethnic roots are not an issue with local Delhi Hindus either who seem to have come to terms with the permanent presence of refugees.[2] The emanating question then is when, how, and why did this twin ethnic amnesia set in? At a more general level, how and when do refugees turn into locals? Is there a correlation between this amnesic self and the distance that needs to be travelled between the identities of refugees and locals? The paradox is hard to miss. While Punjabis in Delhi attempt to distance themselves from their ethnic past, the city has popularly come to be identified as a Punjabi city. This continuously negotiated identification process can perhaps be described as the "Punjabi effect" aggregating the life of the city and its residents, old and new, after the Partition. The "Punjabi effect" sums up a range of discourses that are associated with refugees and the city, particularly the cultural loss associated with the incoming of refugees, the sense of ridicule that accompanies the description of nouveau riche, and the simultaneous ethnic forgetfulness sought by the refugees and their descendants. The roots of this paradox lie not only in the collective episode of forced migration but also the journey of resettlement and social mobility that many of the refugees have travelled over half a century. To unveil the paradox, one needs to understand who were the people that were forced to leave their homes and how did they rebuild their lives. This essay attempts to locate and analyse this "ethnic amnesia" through popular discourses on Punjabi refugees that stem out of personal narratives as well as the State

1
Community leaders, Derawal
Nagar. The common and shared
narratives still provide strong
community bondage to the
refugees from Dera Ismail Khan.

accounts of resettlement. A hegemonic discourse around the theme of last journey and resettlement is created through frequent invocations, ritualized reproductions, and eventual authentication of widespread narratives. The transplantation of popular narratives from personal life histories to official State archives opens hegemonic fields of narration that can be drawn upon to tell "reliable" stories that are not based on mere rumours or hearsay.

To begin with, the tide of forced migration had not started in August 1947, as is popularly believed, but in March 1947 after the Rawalpindi riots. The fall of the Khizar Tiwana government in Punjab following the Muslim League agitation led to widespread riots in Rawalpindi which soon engulfed Lahore, Amritsar, Jhelum, Attock, and Multan.[3] A particular feature of the March violence, besides the unprecedented number of deaths, was the number of people who sought refuge in the camps either because they feared for their safety or their houses had deliberately been burnt. An official estimate from the districts of Attock, Jhelum, and Rawalpindi alone put the number of refugees in the camps at 60,000.[4] The growing uncertainty about the future course of events, such as the drawing of national boundaries, and the possible extent of communal violence, further proved cataclysmic in making people move away to areas perceived as safer, where their community was in the majority. The trickle of refugees in spring had inundated into never-ending columns by the summer of 1947. The exact number of dead, injured, or those forced to migrate in either direction, though, has been a source of contention among historians. Conservative estimates emanating from British sources about the number of casualties put the figure at 2,00,000,[5] while the Indian estimates peg the number at between 4,00,000 and 5,00,000.[6] The estimates in some of the recent studies, that rely on oral historiography extensively, put the figure at 8,00,000.[7] The number of migrants is, thus, equally contested.

2
The Hudson Lines barracks in Kingsway Camp where registered refugees coming from Pakistan were lodged.

3
Derawal Nagar plotted development, the final home for the Dera refugees coming from the transit camps.

For the purpose of this article, population censuses of 1941 and 1951 conducted in Delhi are used to compare the decadal demographic shifts to find the approximate extent of movement. The total population of Delhi in 1941 was counted at 9,17,939 which at an unprecedented decennial growth rate of 106 per cent increased to 17,44,072 in 1951.[8] In absolute numbers, the increase amounts to 1.1 million people, making it the highest ever increase in the city's census history, more so, when the increase does not take into account the outward migration of approximately 3,00,000 Delhi Muslims to Pakistan. Even if we assume that not all the increase was due to the influx of Punjabi refugees owing to the factors of usual rural-urban in-migration, and natural growth rate of 4 per cent, the massive increase can be largely attributed to the Partition-related events.

Following Popular Refugee Discourses

While a range of multiple discourses have emerged around the Punjabi refugees over the decades, a few have taken mythical proportions especially over the widespread narrative of escape and resettlement. Such narratives often are in conflict with the individual narratives but the myths of last journey from Pakistan are so strong that most individuals try to match their stories with the better known narratives. It evolves into a community achieved not through common experiences but common narratives. The popular discourse evolves around the Punjabis themselves and their "indomitable human spirit". The narrations of the flight from West Punjab and the North-West Frontier Province (NWFP) and then the resettlement in Delhi follow a standard theme of destruction and then resurrection through sheer human spirit and endeavour. Though the story remains popular with the first-generation "original migrants", with each passing generation it becomes diluted or further embellished depending on whether the individual/family had a journey upwards or downwards on the ladder of social mobility. The social class and caste play a significant role in how the past is memorized, historicized, and then handed down the generations.

4
Gujranwala Town developed by the government and given as a group housing scheme to the Punjabi refugees.

5
Today colonies like Ramesh Nagar are thriving settlements far removed from the misery of early days of migration.

The same factors help determine how this memory package is received by the subsequent generations. The second related discourse about the Punjabi refugees, at times appears as an appendage, and sometimes as a complete explanation to the success story of refugee rehabilitation. The sources of such eulogy are not the refugees themselves but the State, which in its colonial training of non-partisanship, would normally keep a distance from its subjects. The whispers, rumours, and unwritten stories that form the basis of many discourses, turn "reliable" when they are made available in print through various government publications.

Another noticeable discourse that has emerged over a period but has recently gained wider acceptance is around the "cultural losses" that the city suffered with the influx of refugees. Predictably, this critique stems from a section that describes itself as the "old residents" of Delhi who are contemptuous of the present state where "Tilak Nagars and Nehru Roads proliferate, and hardly anyone knows of the poetry of Mir and Zauq, the humour of Ghalib, the quality of life that Chandni Chowk once symbolized".[9] The cultural nostalgia is not devoid of territory or latent social biases as most of the reminiscences are located around the walled city, British-built New Delhi, or the spacious residential areas of south Delhi.[10] The urban expansion that took place post-Partition has now come to symbolize the loss of high culture and regalia that Delhi once stood for. These "refugee colonies" like Lajpat Nagar, Patel Nagar, Ramesh Nagar, Geeta Colony, etc. are spread all over Delhi and are known for cramped housing and low levels of basic municipal services.

Employing Personal Narratives to Understand Refugee Myths
The purpose in "narrativizing" the well known episodes of Partition migration is to see how some stories have acquired the status of stereotypes or universal accounts that are assumed to have been experienced by all Partition refugees. An insistence on personal

Ravinder Kaur

narrative may sometimes produce gaps that disjoin the personal accounts from the universal ones, thereby challenging the myths built over some decades. But universal accounts are so convenient that many refugees try to replace missing, forgotten parts – or the ones that are too intimate to be disclosed – with borrowed portions from the popular narratives. The conflict between personal and universal narratives does exist but has never been openly displayed. It is interesting in itself to find out how some accounts gain precedence over others. The following narratives will show how contradictory facts cohabit to produce mythical discourses and the most successful discourses are those that gain support from other prevalent discourses stemming from alternate sources.

The north Delhi residential colony of Derawal Nagar is inhabited by refugees from Dera Ismail Khan (DI Khan) in NWFP in Pakistan.[11] The colony was created as a cooperative housing scheme sanctioned by the government for refugees from DI Khan in the late 1950s. The land here, as in many other group housing schemes such as Gujranwala Town, was developed by the State and sold at nominal rates to the members of the DI Khan Sewa Samiti (DI Khan welfare society). Both the organization and the colony are named after the town from which the refugees hailed in Pakistan. In the middle of the colony, a temple has been built on the lines of the temple left behind in DI Khan. A community centre, a homeopathic dispensary,

6
Second-generation inhabitants of Derawal Nagar share their opinions in the Temple Hall.

and a small library have been attached to the temple where prominent members of the society gather every Sunday and on other days of religious importance. The society constitutes upper-caste Khatri families of common descent with most members being part of the same kinship networks. Though structured as an open, democratic organization with a working committee, executive committee, a written constitution with aims and objectives, and a periodic newsletter for its members, it is obvious that membership is bound with caste and religious norms that go beyond the prime condition of past domicile in DI Khan.

The collective narration that follows was presided over by Leela Ram Wadhwa (b. 1919) and K.K. Pahwa (b. 1926), the patriarchs who spoke for everyone else. Their voices were supplemented by others but never contradicted or challenged. Leela Ram as president and Pahwa as his deputy set the precedence in terms of tone, forms of address, and body of thought meant to be conveyed, not only to me as the interviewer, but also to the younger members of the society who had only heard these stories as children. The field of enquiry covered the familiar ground of last journey from Pakistan and rebuilding of homes and lives in this north Delhi suburb.

One of the first popular beliefs that was challenged with this narrative was the ethnic description of refugees as "Punjabis". Leela Ram described himself and the group as Hindu Pathans with a distinct Derawali/Frontier identity. But curiously, this was not a sort of opening definition that preceded the rest of the account, rather an insistence that they were Punjabis like everybody else even though they spoke a different language/dialect from the Punjabis of

7
The active Community Centre at Derawal Nagar.

the plains. The issue was skirted for quite long till Leela Ram started talking of allotment of land to refugee housing societies where he felt that Punjabis had got prime tracts of land while the refugees from DI Khan had to make do with leftover wasteland in north Delhi. This, he continued, despite the fact that the rehabilitation minister at the time of allotment was Mehar Chand Khanna from DI Khan. At some level the discontent simmers but the wider identity of being a Punjabi refugee has been accommodated, though efforts to educate younger generations about their special history have been renewed by the society through various community activities. The recollections were peppered with nostalgic "journeys" of district DI Khan where Hindus formed no more than ten per cent of the total population of 2,98,131.[12] The town of DI Khan was described as the town of temples, the "Kashi of the Frontier"[13] where Hindus lived respectably in one half of the town while Muslims occupied the rest. The town was a trading junction and the last point of transit for goods on the way to Afghanistan and Central Asia. Most Hindus and Sikhs were traders by profession, had substantial landholdings, and almost all of them vaguely described their families as being "well-to-do". This self perception about their socio-economic profile in pre-Partition Punjab and NWFP is echoed elsewhere as well where they are described as "urban, lower/middle class whose main occupations were that of merchants, bankers, moneylenders, professionals, and teachers".[14] The urban-middle class profile of the incoming refugees is further confirmed in a number of quantitative studies conducted later in Delhi city.[15]

"Detailing" the Narratives

While the background of the community and its glorious past in DI Khan was illustrated with examples from Leela Ram's and K.K. Pahwa's family histories, they turned to P.L. Kataria (b. 1934) to describe their struggle after forced migration from DI Khan. Kataria told me that he had travelled in a crowded train along with his family and arrived at Delhi railway station where his family was given refugee registration numbers and place to live in Hudson Lines barracks in Kingsway Camp. He had to do odd jobs for survival like selling vegetables, manual labour, and filling up ration forms for illiterate refugees on their arrival in Delhi. Then Kataria got a job in the army and later in a government department as a clerk from where he recently retired. All this was told in a matter-of-fact manner, without any vivid recollections or silent pauses that are so closely associated with narration of personal histories.[16] One could, perhaps, consider it as an example of a gendered mode of narration of personal histories. Or was it an inevitable pitfall of collective narration presided over by community patriarchs where the narratives become repetitive, rehearsed, and ritualized. In any case, vivid details were considered irrelevant by the group where the idea seemed to be to construct an account that reiterated the earlier stated unique characteristics of the community such as *gairat* (pride or self respect), ability to work hard, and strong loyalty like their Muslim Pathan counterparts. An insistence on hearing the irrelevant details produced confusion, impatience, and even friendly warnings of losing focus.

Kataria was one of the many refugees who came empty-handed and rebuilt their lives from scratch, embodying the true human spirit. While it is not always possible to challenge stereotypes, it is possible to construct a fuller and a unique individual account by asking for finer details. One vital detail here was the manner in which camp allotments were made. Kataria recalled that on arrival at Delhi railway station (now called Old Delhi railway station, near Kashmere Gate), refugees would go to the refugee registration office situated in a nearby building called Wavell Canteen. They would be given refugee registration numbers and asked if they needed food and clothing rations from the State. The answer, yes or no, would then form the basis for allotment of barracks or cloth tents in various camps. The ones who could afford their own rations would be allotted Hudson and Reeds Lines barracks, while those who could not would be sent to Edward and Outram Lines. The latter would be housed in cloth tents, surplus from World War II, while the former were settled in concrete barracks. Though this is a small detail, it tells us about those refugees who had their own means of survival, i.e. those who had brought along some capital saved for hard times. Kataria's family was settled in Hudson Lines suggesting that they did not come entirely empty handed and had some means to fall back upon.

It was still not clear why K.K. Pahwa and Leela Ram turned away from their personal life stories to fill in the last journey from DI Khan to Delhi. How did they experience that mythical journey and why were they reluctant to narrate it? Leela Ram described his story as irrelevant and in no way connected with my research of refugees. The prime reason was that he had migrated to Delhi in 1946 much before Partition. He further narrated:

"My family was long established in the trading business in DI Khan. In 1936 some British officers distributed a pamphlet asking the Hindus in DI Khan to choose a place where they would like to migrate in the event of Partition between India and Pakistan. So, my father chose Delhi while many others chose other Hindu cities like Lahore and Amritsar in Punjab. Finally in 1946 my father sent me to Delhi to purchase a shop and establish an independent business. When the trouble started in Punjab, the rest of my family moved here as well. We later helped many others from DI Khan to move here and organized relief for them."

Surely, Leela Ram's experience was very different from Kataria's in that he had made the journey long before anyone else had anticipated Partition. Even though it is difficult to connect the "pamphlet distributed by British officers" with any such known actual event, it is clear that some people were definitely entertaining the thought of leaving for perceived safer areas. The date ascribed to the distribution of the pamphlet is historically unlikely because it was in 1936 that the idea of Pakistan was generated for the first time by a group of Indian Muslim students at Oxford. The idea was never taken seriously until Jinnah reincarnated it as the famous "two-nation theory" in 1940 at Lahore. So the question of making a choice between India and Pakistan in 1936 simply did not arise.

Pahwa, on the other hand, recalled the efforts that he undertook to locate his younger brother in DI Khan while most of his family had already moved to Alwar and Delhi in April 1947. He was 21 years old at that time and had to stay back to look after the family property and to evacuate his brother. "The superintendent of police was a Muslim officer who would not allow us to take anything away. I had to negotiate with him for everything and we were not feeling safe even in our own house. As the situation worsened we decided to leave. We bought two plane tickets and flew to Delhi where we already had family." Pahwa's story was also "different" in that he flew to safety and did not experience intimately the perils of travelling on trains or by road. And when asked about the "Partition journey" he would normally refer to widespread narratives but never his own. Both he and Leela Ram described their migratory experiences as irrelevant and then pointed to others who had experienced the more commonly used modes of journey. In a way, they seemed compelled to attune their experiences to the better known ones as if they had been robbed of the glory attached to the popular narratives.

From these narratives, it is clear that there was more than one form of capital that the refugees had accumulated and transplanted to Delhi. If one proceeded with Bourdieu's identification of types of capitals[17] – social, cultural, financial – that are generated through affiliations with educational and other elite institutions, expansion of social networks etc. and that can only be built up through generations, then one can understand why some refugees needed State support and others did not. Even for someone like Kataria, whose personal narrative came closest to the popular ones, the journey to resettlement was more complicated than the popular accounts. From his account, one can hazard a guess that his family belonged to the latter group not only in terms of some savings transformed as financial capital but also in terms of capital gained through education which enabled him to earn a living and maintain his self-supporting status. The profits earned from such in/visible capital enabled many like him to reiterate their self-respect and male pride that later formed the basis for some of the mythical accounts about refugees.

Another finer detail that challenged the popular refugee perception was the account of Kataria's efforts at gaining employment. The initial phase, where he had attempted odd jobs, was replete with minor anecdotes and related episodes whereas the latter part where he gained a permanent job was bereft of description. It was presumed to be too ordinary for mention as it had little to do with the general theme of struggle successfully waged by the refugees. The detail of State assistance could rob the long-established glory since Kataria had benefited from the relaxed rules and employment policy practices of the government. The government had announced a number of provisions concerning refugee employment as early as 1948. This included increase in the age limit for application to State jobs from 25 to 40 for refugees; a lenient view of educational qualifications, for example, a candidate who had failed the class 10 exam or passed class 8 would be considered the equivalent of a matriculate; creation of employment exchanges or job data banks for the refugees; work training centres within refugee camps, for example in Kingsway and Arab-ki-Sarai;[18] exemption of training requirements of teachers;[19] establishment of a transfer bureau for refugees who were previously employed by the State and who now were displaced from Pakistan and sought new jobs. Those students who could not take exams due to violent disturbances were given certificates in lieu of social service rendered in refugee camps. These certificates could then be used to strengthen claims for employment or admission to educational institutions. In April

8
Narratives, customs, and beliefs continue to be shared between generations. Delhi parks provide a haven for community get-togethers.

9

Sarojini Nagar market where many Punjabi refugees rebuilt their homes and families by starting stalls that eventually became shops.

1948, the Ministry of Rehabilitation asked the state governments to exclusively reserve all vacancies created by the displacement of Muslims for the refugees.[20] The Ministry of Railways even agreed to reserve 15,000 vacancies in grades III–IV for the displaced people, while the Ministry of Industry and Supply agreed to allot additional quotas of steel to create greater employment opportunities for them.[21]

State Authenticates Popular Discourse

The relationship between the State and the refugees is quite engaging. Most of the State efforts at resettlement rarely find mention in the personal stories, though the State pays unceasing homage to the grit and resolution of the Punjabi refugees. The State becomes the second source of the same discourse, namely, the human spirit of the Punjabis. The most telling metaphor for Punjabi refugees was used by M.S. Randhawa who, during the early years of Independence, was Director General of Rehabilitation in Punjab. He equated Punjabis with Tahli, a hardwood tree commonly found in Punjab. He told the story of Tahli trees uprooted by the outgoing Muslim refugees for fuel, which were mutilated so badly that only stumps were left in two columns along the Grand Trunk Road. It seemed as if the road would have to be replanted. After three years these stumps got covered with luxuriant leafy branches again. "How symbolic of people the Tahli tree is! Like Phoenix, the mythical bird...who after burning itself on a funeral pyre, rose again from its ashes, young and vigorous, Punjab is born again after undergoing a terrible ordeal, which would have destroyed a weaker race."[22]

The other authoritative state account is an official publication called *The Story of Rehabilitation* which describes migration and resettlement in a familiar vein of death, destruction, and resurrection. The inevitable episodes of leaving home are reconstructed passionately:

"Huge masses of people were gripped with fear. You could see it in glazed eyes staring into vacancy. No hope of survival in the homes of their forefathers. They faced dangers worse than death. This brutality in the name of religion was in truth a perversion of it. The injunction was to kill, kill, kill. And the victims of hate, what could they do but flee in their hundreds of thousands."[23]

The ones who did manage to escape are described as "people crazed with fear, shattered in body and mind, most of them pitifully destitute".[24] While laying a preface to the resettlement issues, the State magnanimously shares the credit for successful rehabilitation:

Ravinder Kaur

"It rebounds to the eternal credit of displaced persons from West Pakistan. Their toughness, their sturdy sense of self reliance, their pride that would not submit to the indignity of living on dole and charity never shone as they did in this hour of supreme trial. Tens of thousands of them disdained government help. They carried on regardless of the inclemencies of the weather with a stoicism that took our breath away. Remember, hundreds of them had seen affluent days in the homes they had abandoned."[25]

Then, to illustrate the struggle and pride, the document narrates a story that is often told as an example of Punjabi spirit. Only this time, it gains the authenticity of the printed word, and that too in the State chronicle:

"There is the poignant story of a young Punjabi lad hawking newspapers in New Delhi's fashionable shopping centre. On a generous impulse a kindly soul offered him a rupee-note in exchange for a paper and waived the proffered change. There were tears in the youngster's eyes as he angrily protested that he was not a beggar. Here was a gallantry that mocked at adversity and would never admit defeat."[26]

This story has further been authenticated through repeated references in scholarly works on Punjabi refugees in Delhi. For example, V.N. Dutta, a renowned historian and a refugee himself reproduced the entire story as evidence of Punjabi spirit in his essay "Punjabi Refugees and the Urban Development of Greater Delhi".[27] The same story is recounted in official and unofficial accounts innumerable times to make this point. Even a socio-economic study commissioned by the Planning Commission to measure the scale and impact of sudden demographics in Delhi after Partition could not escape the stereotypes. The study was conducted by the well known economist from Delhi University, V.K.R.V. Rao who paid "high tributes to the spirit of enterprise and the hard work of the refugee population".[28] Almost as an afterthought the author adds, "besides, of course, [the successful resettlement is]...attributable to their higher academic qualifications and skills" and "in part, due to the help they received from the government in respect of their residential and business accommodation, and to a smaller extent, to the special educational and financial facilities they received from the government".[29]

Claiming Locality

By the 1960s most of the resettlement work among the Partition refugees was deemed to have been finished by the government. The resettlement was considered successful "only when the displaced person has shed his own dependence on government or private doles".[30] The benchmark of refugee independence was measured with their ability to provide for themselves and their families, and whether they had "a roof over their head".[31] The goal of providing a roof over every head was fulfilled through mass construction projects in and around Delhi, especially the massive Faridabad project in the National Capital Region. The city itself had expanded to an extent that new administrative districts, south and west Delhi, had to be carved out in 1953. As early as 1954, a change was reported in the Delhi landscape where the city seemed to be spreading endlessly, new colonies were springing up everywhere, each one equipped with a market or shopping centre and provided with ample amenities. To a visitor who had last witnessed the Delhi landscape in the dark days of 1949 the transformation must have had a breathtaking quality. New colonies throbbed with a vigorous life. The misery and the squalor of the early days of migration had been all but erased from memory.[32]

The colonies referred to here include Ramesh Nagar, Tilak Nagar, Subhash Nagar, Moti Nagar, Patel Nagar, in west Delhi; Lajpat Nagar, Jangpura, Bhogal, Malviya Nagar in south Delhi; and Geeta Colony, Gandhi Nagar, Krishna Nagar in east Delhi. At the same time, private plots were developed by the Ministry of Rehabilitation in conjunction with other local government bodies, in areas like Safdarjung Enclave, South Extension, Rajouri Garden, Punjabi Bagh, Kirti Nagar, for sale to those refugees who had received substantial compensation for property lost in Pakistan. The other goal of economic independence was pursued through creation of liberal conditions of eligibility for State employment, grant of easy loans for private businesses, and training and provision of other vocational education. A large part of the five-year plan allocations was diverted to refugee employment schemes. An estimated Rs 6 crore was spent within the First Plan while another Rs 2 crore was earmarked for the Second Plan. The specially constituted Rehabilitation Finance Administration had sanctioned 10,000 easy loans.[33] To create an economy around refugees several commercial complexes were established in Sarojini Nagar, Khan Market, Lajpat Rai Market, Janpath, Central Market in Lajpat Nagar, where shops were allotted to refugees at nominal rents.[34]

In 1965, these goals towards refugee rehabilitation were deemed to have been met and the ministry itself was abolished and turned into a division of the Union Home Ministry. This, in a way, closed the two-decade-long chapter of refugee resettlement. In Derawal Nagar, similar sentiments were expressed when K.K. Pahwa tried to fix a date for their irreversible journey from refugee to local status in Delhi. He invoked the now-familiar theme of Punjabi pride in tandem with an episode that supposedly turned them into locals. "It started with complaints about locals in Delhi who never supported us. They used to call us 'Sharnarthis', the refugees. It sounded like an abuse because we were used to giving charity to others, not receiving it. All of us had big businesses at Dera Ismail Khan. And we had self-respect and pride, just like Pathans. We worked hard to get rid of this 'refugee' title. Some of us got small jobs, others became hawkers or petty traders buying and selling on a day-to-day basis. But we never begged from anybody and never sat down to lament our fate. It was God's will that we were displaced. Later, some big officers came to visit us and said that we were not 'Sharnarthi' but 'Purusharthi', the able-bodied men who were capable of doing the impossible. Earlier we had to write 'refugee' in every official document, but in 1965 we refused to be called so. We had shops, houses, jobs, and a lifestyle better than the locals, so why should we accept being called refugees."

The attempt to fix a date on the change of status from refugee to local is rather significant since such transformations are gradual and take place over long periods of time. More significantly, fixing of the date is not sought by the State but the refugees themselves. The change in status is attributed to an official source where after a visit or inspection they were pronounced non-refugees by the State representatives. It was a sort of official blessing that transformed them dramatically into non-refugees, giving them a status which was perceived as more respectable than that of those located in refugee camps. Exemption from mentioning their "refugee" status after the 1965 closure of the ministry is seen as a point of no-return both by the State and the refugees. Here, the power of State documents filters deep into the psyche of State subjects, entwined as they are, with the imagination of citizenship. The innocuous-looking forms, schemes in triplicate, and the identities they construct and confer on individuals represent the power matrix which the State and its subjects continue to cohabit in contemporary Delhi.

NOTES

1.   See Ravi Dayal, "A Kayastha's View", in *Seminar* No. 515, July 2002, p. 21.

2.   The lack of local vs migrant conflict in Delhi becomes significant when contrasted with Sindhi-Muhajir conflict in Karachi city in Pakistan. Karachi drew a substantial Muslim refugee population from north-central India during Partition and the refugees got embroiled in an unceasing violent conflict.

3.   For details see Anders Bjørn Hansen, *Partition and Genocide: Manifestations of Violence in Punjab 1937–47*, Delhi, 2002, pp. 109–13.

4.   Hansen, *Partition and Genocide*, p. 113.

5.   Penderel Moon, *Divide and Quit*, 1961, reprint Delhi, 1998.

6. G.D. Khosla, *Stern Reckoning: A Survey of Events Leading up to and Following the Partition of India,* 1950, reprint New Delhi, 1989.

7. Urvashi Butalia, *The Other Side of Silence: Voices from the Partition of India,* New Delhi,1998.

8. Census of India, 1941 and 1951.

9. Narayani Gupta, *Delhi Between Two Empires 1803–1931: Society, Government and Urban Growth,* Delhi, 1999, quoted from the preface of the first edition printed in 1981.

10. See for example the July 2002 issue of the monthly journal *Seminar* entitled "First City?" where most of the participants in their first-person memoirs narrate the idyll that Delhi was, the shaded boulevards of the new city, the lights and bazaars of Old Delhi, and the upper-class cosmopolitan life of south Delhi. There is no mention of the nondescript areas that were developed after Partition, except some areas of south Delhi, where the bulk of the population now lives.

11. Group interview with members of the working committee, Dera Ismail Khan Sewa Samiti, Derawal Nagar on December 7, 2000.

12. See District Population in NWFP, Census of India, 1941.

13. M.S. Randhawa, *Out of Ashes: An Account of the Rehabilitation of Refugees from West Pakistan in Rural Areas of Punjab,* Chandigarh, 1954.

14. Randhawa, *Out of Ashes;* also see Richard Fox's description of Punjabi Hindus in the Introduction, *Lions of Punjab: Culture of Making,* Berkeley, 1985.

15. V.K.R.V. Rao and N.B. Desai, *Greater Delhi: A Study in Urbanization, 1940–57,* New Delhi, 1965.

16. For example note Butalia's account of her interviews with female survivors of Partition in *The Other Side of Silence.*

17. See Annual Report 1947–48, Ministry of Relief and Rehabilitation, Government of India.

18. See AICC Papers (II Instalment) about various work training centres run separately for men and women.

19. Mohanlal Saxena, *Some Reflections on the Problems of Rehabilitation,* Delhi, 1950, p. 51. M.L. Saxena was Minister for Relief and Rehabilitation 1948–50.

20. Saxena, *Some Reflections,* p. 51.

21. Saxena, *Some Reflections,* p. 42.

22. Randhawa, *Out of Ashes,* p. 223.

23. U. Bhaskar Rao, *The Story of Rehabilitation,* Delhi, 1967, p. 5.

24. Rao, *The Story of Rehabilitation,* p. 36.

25. Rao, *The Story of Rehabilitation,* p. 37.

26. Rao, *The Story of Rehabilitation,* p. 37.

27. See V.N. Dutta's essay in R.E. Frykenberg, ed., *Delhi through the Ages: Essays in Urban History, Culture and Society,* Delhi, 1986.

28. Rao and Desai, *Greater Delhi,* p. xx.

29. Rao and Desai, *Greater Delhi,* p. xx.

30. Rao, *The Story of Rehabilitation,* p. 62.

31. Rao, *The Story of Rehabilitation,* p. 62.

32. Rao, *The Story of Rehabilitation,* p. 62.

33. Easy loans meant no interest payable for the first year and 3 1/8 per cent per annum thereafter. Rao, *The Story of Rehabilitation,* p. 67.

34. For example, the monthly rent in Khan Market was Rs 50. This information is based on a survey that I conducted among shopkeepers in Khan Market in December 2000.

Suneetha Dasappa Kacker

The DDA and
the Idea of Delhi

Delhi, 1947–57

In 1947, Delhi emerged as the governing centre of four hundred million people – the capital city of a country struggling to come to terms with the upheavals surrounding its new independence. The city itself was undergoing a sea-change, under tremendous pressures: a flow of refugees, displaced from Pakistan, were entering Delhi. These increased with phenomenal rapidity to a flood of five lakh people. Simultaneously, the exclusion of Lahore from the country after Partition was precipitating a redistribution of commerce and wholesale trade patterns in northern India. Trade and commerce gravitated towards Delhi, and Old Delhi – already congested and under strain – in particular. Also, as the national capital, Delhi attracted an influx of administrative and bureaucratic establishments – the apparatus of the State, foreign missions, as well as institutional bodies.

Multiple agencies operated in this context, in an effort to restore a semblance of order in the city. While a substantial number of refugee families took shelter in properties vacated by those who had left the country, the Ministry of Rehabilitation began operations on a war footing to cater to the rest: the government acquired large areas of raw land on the outskirts of Delhi – at times almost on its undeveloped peripheral edges – to build rehabilitation colonies. By 1950, nearly twenty colonies, covering about 3,000 acres, were opened up, officially accommodating about two lakh refugees. About 930 acres were developed in the west, 241 in the north, and 2.6 in the east. The largest acreage developed – encompassing Nizamuddin, Jangpura, Lajpat Nagar, Kalkaji, and Malviya Nagar – was in the south, redefining the southern limits of the existing city.

Simultaneously, the Delhi Improvement Trust was active in and around the Old City, opening new areas for its extension, in order to relieve congestion and control haphazard suburban development. Under its schemes, wild and barren lands to the west and northwest of Delhi, inhabited by Gujjars and other tribal communities, were being "transformed into beautiful middle class residential suburbs, with one or two storeyed buildings".[1] These extensions, the largest of which was the Shadipur Town Expansion Scheme, together covered an area of roughly 2,800 acres, and accounted for a large part of the city's expansion to the west.

1 & 2
Housing and commercial facilities in Rohini – the tour de force of the DDA's efforts at master planning through speculation.

Alongside these agencies, private land colonizing companies were also acquiring and developing large tracts of agricultural land for residential uses. Their efforts were concentrated in the southern and western edges of the city; and the price at which land was sold – ranging from Rs 10 to Rs 20 per square yard – made it reasonably affordable to the middle and upper income groups. These companies flourished due to the abnormally high demand for land from the refugees.

None of these efforts, however, could cater sufficiently for the growing numbers of low income households in the city. As a result, squatting on vacant government lands was on the increase; and substandard residential developments were mushrooming at a rapid rate, especially on the highways leading to the capital. These were becoming popular and established forms of residential development for a substantial segment of the city's population.

By the mid-1950s, Delhi had become a sprawling city of about two million inhabitants, marked by gaping inequities in standards of development and sharp social boundaries: the walled city, suffering from extreme overcrowding, housed low and middle income households; New Delhi, characterized by spaciousness and green vistas, was taken over by the government and its functionaries; private and public residential developments, plotted at medium densities, and offering wholesome environments, catered to the fairly well-off; and unserviced squatter and illegal settlements housed the poor. The city had grown rapidly, and in an unbalanced way, in the south and the west.

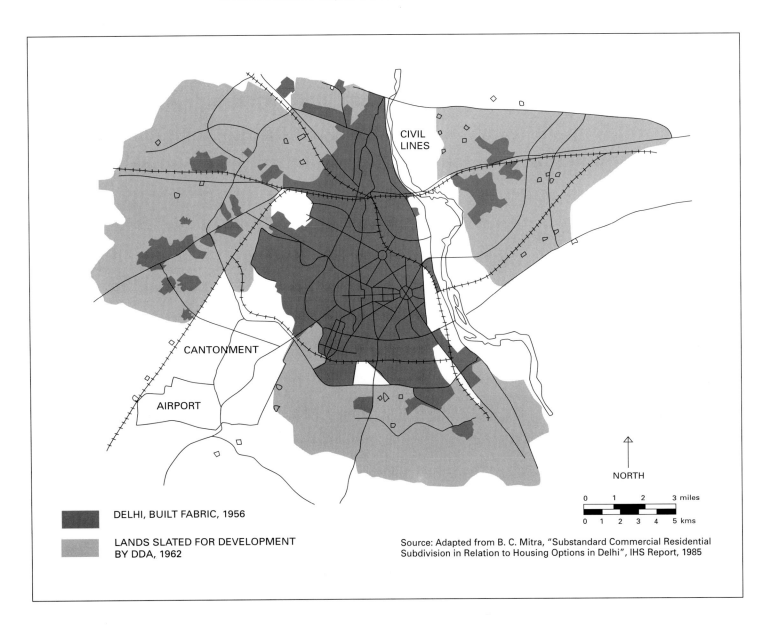

■ DELHI, BUILT FABRIC, 1956

■ LANDS SLATED FOR DEVELOPMENT
BY DDA, 1962

Source: Adapted from B. C. Mitra, "Substandard Commercial Residential Subdivision in Relation to Housing Options in Delhi", IHS Report, 1985

At this stage, the need for a coherent development strategy to control and direct the growth of the metropolis became exigent. A committee in 1954 recommended the setting up of a single planning and controlling authority for urban Delhi as a whole, pointing out that neither had a civic survey been undertaken, nor a Master Plan prepared for the city as yet.

As a result, the Delhi Development Authority (DDA) was constituted on December 30, 1957, through an Act of Parliament called the Delhi Development Act. It was envisaged as the apex planning authority for the city. Thereafter, in 1958, the Municipal Corporation of Delhi, responsible for various support and service functions, was set up. Together, these represented the state's earliest attempts at the integrated planning and development of urban areas in the country. The DDA's initial mandate was "to promote and secure the development of Delhi through a civic survey and a Master Plan".[2]

Urban Intervention and the Indian State

Almost without exception, accounts of public planning authorities in developing countries throw up the same conclusions: a gross mismatch between what is projected – and officially stated – and what is achieved on ground. The purpose here is not simply to add to these descriptions of projected targets and shortfalls, but to provide some insights into the dynamics of city development in the context of India's capital city; to situate the DDA, as the main instrument of city planning, within the social, economic, and above all, political realities of its time.

Thus, while Delhi was expanding in an uncontrolled manner, the Greater Delhi Survey in 1956 revealed that 82 per cent of the households in the city earned less than Rs 250 per month. This established that the large majority of households did not earn enough to pay the economic rent of even a single-room dwelling unit – estimated at about Rs 30 – at the time. These findings were reflected in the First Five-Year Plan, which concluded that "private enterprise is not in a position to do the job (of ensuring access to urban amenities) as far as the low income groups are concerned. They cannot afford to pay the economic rent for housing accommodation of even the minimum standards."[3] That the State would have to play a very direct and substantial role in restraining speculative interests, and enabling equitable access to urban facilities, became evident to the nation's leaders. Above all, land was perceived as the resource to be controlled in order to regulate the market, and ensure equitable development within the guidelines laid down by a Master Plan.

To a large extent, these perceptions for the development of urban areas, and of Delhi in particular, were an extension of the strategies for overall development adopted by the Indian State soon after Independence. At the time, industrial and commercial groups in the country were fairly weak, and favoured protectionism and State intervention to ensure their consolidation. This stand was supported by the dominant political interest, which was committed to transforming India into a modern industrial society. Ideologically, however, great emphasis was laid on integrating social goals with economic development, i.e. on the redistribution of economic benefits to enable the upliftment of the mass of the population. It was perceived that the State would have to play a strong role in ensuring this. As a result, the pattern of development opted for favoured indirect State participation in support of private enterprise – implying State ownership of key productive assets; and planning for growth and redistribution.

Planning called for the creation of a large bureaucracy of economic and technical personnel, to monitor and direct State programmes. Derived from the already existing colonial administrative bureaucracy, this sector spread rapidly in size, and increased its control over productive processes and assets, resulting in the growth of a large non-market mechanism of resource allocation – a process justified by arguments of controlling private profiteering, and enabling redistribution and greater social justice.

3
District Centres such as this one in East Delhi were provided in all the Master Plans of the DDA. Their speculative nature and dated concept destined them to degradation within a decade. Photograph courtesy the writer.

These processes were mirrored in the modes of intervention that the State adopted for the regulation and planning of Delhi. It sought primarily to act as an instrument of control over urban resources – mainly land – in order to enable a greater socialization of the city. Thus, even while the DDA was in the process of preparing a Master Plan for the city, the government announced a freeze on all vacant undeveloped land within the urbanizable limits. The intention to acquire all such lands was announced as early as 1957, and legal notices were served to the effect in 1959.

The policy of large-scale acquisition and development of land aimed at creating a land bank that would facilitate the realization of the Master Plan proposals by making land available "in adequate quantities, at the right times and at reasonable prices to both public authorities and individuals".[4] Establishing itself as the sole agency legally authorized to develop and dispose of land, the State left little, or no role for the private land developer – seeking, thereby, to eliminate speculation, and enable the optimal social use of land. 62,200 acres were proposed to be acquired between 1961 and 1981. The cost of acquisition was to be met out of a revolving fund established for the purpose, in which revenues from the sale of developed land would be re-circulated to purchase and develop more land. All land would be made available to users on a 99-year lease, in accordance with the land-use plan enunciated in the Master Plan. The policy was to be administered by the DDA, which was also mandated to implement the Master Plan. Delhi thus became the first city in the world where land banking through State intervention was attempted on a large scale.

4 & 5
The low and middle income housing projects have provided enormous benefits for those who could access them. Photographs courtesy the writer.

The City for Everybody...

If the image of Shahjahan's city was as a garden of paradise; and that of the British capital a reflection of imperial power; so the projection of Delhi under the new State was as a city for everybody: an arena where all would find adequate representation, irrespective of social or economic power. This was the promise held by the unprecedented and large-scale State intervention that the city witnessed from 1959 onwards.

The land earmarked for acquisition was to be developed and auctioned for commercial and industrial uses, and partly for residential uses, with profits being used to subsidize the costs of developments for the low-income groups. The overall pattern of development for the city was detailed in the Master Plan document. The Plan itself was guided by highly pragmatic considerations, in view of the prevailing social and economic context. It emphasized the need to restrain the size of the city's population, so as to keep its growth within manageable limits. It sought also to relate the location of work centres to residential areas, in order to rationalize transportation; and to synthesize the city, by progressively equalizing living conditions, and redistributing densities in the Old City, New Delhi, and in the Civil Lines area. It proposed to achieve this partly through a massive public housing programme, aimed largely at the middle and lower income groups. The Master Plan proposals, along with the urban land policy were thus intended as a comprehensive package aimed at the balanced growth of the city.

These instruments of city planning, formulated and legislated under Nehru, reflect his ideal of the State as an arbitrator and redistributive agent in development. They acknowledge that the requirements of long-term urban strategy and the legitimation of planning processes in a poor country necessitate an effective redistributive programme that addresses the needs of the large numbers of the underprivileged. In other words, the success of the Master Plan, in a context such as Delhi's, was seen contingent upon the inclusion of all segments of the population in the processes of city development. Great store was laid on the land policy, as a measure that would enable this.

Paradoxically, however, the very organizational characteristics of Nehru's party – the Congress – undermined the effective implementation of any redistributive policies pursued through institutional channels. The Congress, as the major political force at the time, played a leading role in shaping State politics and interventions for development. While the party was led by a modern intelligentsia which was ideologically inclined towards reform, its organizational structure relied primarily on established local leaders – dominant landlords, merchants, and businessmen – to organize mass support for national policies. This tendency helped preserve and strengthen established patterns of dominance.[5] In effect, the party was unable to detach or distance itself from the existing social order, so as to re-order it. As a result, the dominant or propertied classes were powerful in local State institutions and civic

6 *below left*
For those who could not get DDA housing, the private developers obliged by colonizing green fields with unauthorized housing. Photograph courtesy the writer.

7 *below right*
For those who could not access unauthorized housing the slumlords provided space for shelters. Photograph courtesy the writer.

8
The DDA main office. In addition it houses its complex and large organization in a number of decentralized offices that facilitate easy public access.

establishments, and, in general, the legislation of progressive reform policies had minimal effect. This was validated by the dismal performance of the rural land reform programmes initiated soon after Independence.

In the urban situation, it could also be argued that the success of the land policy would have rested on an elaborate, efficient, and well organized bureaucracy, which the country lacked at the time. Nonetheless, what becomes patently obvious is the absence of political ability on the part of the State to redistribute either existing resources, or the benefits of its interventions in a more equitable manner than that determined by the traditional distribution of power. In the face of the State's inability to implement its programme, the bureaucratic elite – and, as they became politicized, the politicians – gradually assumed immense control over the urban sphere.

The State as Speculator

The sale of land developed by the DDA for private housing began only in 1964, five years after the land freeze. Although the policy for disposal had envisaged the distribution of at least half of the plots developed to the low income groups on the basis of lots, in actual practice the emphasis was on open auctions, to which only the rich had access. Priority was clearly given to maximizing profits through the sale of land at high prices: land was released in a staggered manner, and plots in developed areas were deliberately withheld, to push prices up. While this was done on the pretext of raising funds to meet the costs of development for the poor, even a decade after its operation, barely 11 per cent of the plots developed had reached the lower income groups. Until 1975, up to half of the plots developed by the Authority in prime locations had been auctioned. The DDA and the land development programme thus catered overwhelmingly to the rich.

Suneetha Dasappa Kacker

Meanwhile, the Authority largely ignored its public housing programme in the initial few years. This was begun only in 1966, seven years after the land freeze, and consisted of built-up units provided on a hire-purchase basis to lower and middle income group families. Supply, however, fell far short of the demand – by 1980 only about 50,000 units had been completed, satisfying only 44 per cent of the registered demand.[6] This despite the fact that the high costs, lengthy and complicated administrative procedures, and the lack of choice deterred a large number of applicants in need of housing.

Similarly, the DDA, vested with monopoly powers of development, was unable to meet people's requirements for commercial and work places. Of the fifteen District Centres proposed in the Master Plan, barely a fifth had been developed and were operational in 1980; only one of the 23 flatted factory estates recommended in the Plan had been built.

In the interim, the freezing of land within practically the entire urbanizable limits, and the government's inability, thereafter, to make developed land available rapidly and at reasonable prices, led to an artificial scarcity of land in the city. This drove land prices up prohibitively. Between 1959 and 1970, land prices in Delhi increased by up to a thousand per cent in some localities where freehold land that had not been notified for acquisition was still available. Caught between the DDA's indifference, and sky-rocketing land prices, the lower- and middle-income groups found that they could neither live, nor work, within the legal framework in the city. The situation was aptly summed up by Ashish Bose, in a report in 1969:

"The DDA has frozen the land, and whatever they developed took years and years; and even then, much of it was auctioned at very high prices, and the plots which were allotted by draw of lots could not possibly meet the growing demand for housing. In desperation, the poor and middle class people of Delhi bought land in unauthorised colonies, and built unauthorised structures by the thousands."[7]

9
The network of parks developed by the DDA, such as this one at Rohini, has been exemplary in providing a healthy environment in their development projects.

"In Delhi, they sell land on blueprint like cinema tickets."[8]

Before 1962, 110 unauthorized colonies already existed in Delhi. These were regularized when the Master Plan for the city was officially notified. However, the land freeze of 1959, and the subsequent nature of developments in the city gave further impetus to the formation of these colonies, so that between 1962 and 1967, a further 101 illegal settlements had sprung up. Spreading like wildfire, their numbers had increased to 471 in 1977. By 1981, they occupied nearly 3,000 hectares of land – a third of the area proposed for residential use in the Master Plan. Ironically, the official land policy, meant to facilitate the implementation of the Master Plan, led, instead, to the proliferation of unauthorized structures at a faster rate than before.

Thus, at the conclusion of the Plan's twenty-year perspective period in 1982, many of its proposals for the controlled development of the city were no longer feasible. Illegal settlements already occupied land intended for district centres, community facilities, open spaces, residential and industrial uses. The underlying causes that led to this situation have not been rectified or mitigated in successive plans or policy measures. On the other hand, the continued exclusion of large segments of the population from institutional mechanisms of access to the urban sphere has spawned a system of patronage that has infiltrated the processes of planning and resource allocation. Where the DDA was unable, or unwilling, to deliver, illegal colonizers, and well-connected patrons enabled access to land, services, and economic prospects to the poor in the city. The weakening of political regimes after 1978 further intensified and perpetuated this trend – politicians as patrons were able to offer concrete benefits in the city in exchange for electoral support, thus building up large vote banks based on informal transfers of resources that effectively subverted the formal processes of planning and allocation. The politicization of the bureaucracy and key urban institutions facilitated and further promoted the system. With policies aimed at ensuring political returns,

10

As the pressure of population growth increases, more recent developments such as Dwarka begin to densify their fabric. The absence of an urban vision continues to take its toll on the city.

Suneetha Dasappa Kacker

rather than the beneficial development of the city itself, Delhi has increasingly been used as an element of political capital making.

While its planning functions have been subverted, the DDA has been successful in undertaking large projects in the city. In the twenty years following 1980, the Authority has built sports facilities, cultural centres, district and community centres; and developed industrial estates and parks in the city. It has also improved upon the delivery of built-up housing units to all segments of the population. These are sited in pockets within the city's built fabric, as well as in entire subcities, meant as urban extension areas: Rohini, Dwarka, and Narela, together covering over 17,000 hectares, and meant to accommodate a million people each. In spite of the drawbacks associated with them – the lack of choice, long waiting periods, and poor quality of construction – the DDA's housing programme undoubtedly offers a much needed and affordable option to the city's middle and lower income groups. Moreover, the planning parameters and standards adopted in these developments compare favourably with those common in private developments of a similar nature.

The DDA is probably among the most prolific urban development authorities in the world today – having undertaken projects of a magnitude seldom conceived of in any other city. This project-based approach to development, however, fails to address the underlying paradox that planning efforts for the city must confront: How can the aspirations of 70 per cent of the urban population for economic and social betterment in the city be enabled, without antagonizing the more established segments of society? What conditions will create the context for the successful legislation of coherent policies towards these groups? It is in these issues that the next vision for Delhi must be rooted.

NOTES

1.   A. Bopegamage, *Delhi – A Study in Urban Sociology,* University of Bombay Press, 1957, p. 93.

2.   E.F.N. Ribeiro, "Urban Land Policies in the Context of the Development Plan for Delhi", paper presented at the seminar on Land in Metropolitan Development, Calcutta, 1982, p. 4.

3.   M. Mehta, "Housing Policies in India: Retrospect and Prospect", undated mimeo, School of Planning, Ahmedabad, p. 6.

4.   Ribeiro,"Urban Land Policies", p. 2.

5.   F. Frankel, *India's Political Economy: 1947–1977: The Gradual Revolution,* Princeton University Press, 1978, pp. 18–23.

6.   B.C. Mitra, "Substandard Commercial Residential Subdivisions in Relation to Housing Options in Delhi", Report No. 966, 41st ICHPB, 1985, p. 27.

7.   A. Bose, *Land Speculation in Urban Delhi,* Institute for Economic Growth, Delhi, 1969, p. 28.

8.   Official of the MCD, on unauthorized settlements, quoted in Bose, *Land Speculation*, p. 2.

Véronique Dupont

The Idea of a New Chic Delhi through Publicity Hype

The great escape. Get away to a whole new experience.
The Zodiac of your life. A whole new world of gracious living.

At first glance what is the connection between these two promotional slogans? The first, exhorting the reader to make a "great escape" as the start to a "whole new experience", could be an invitation to travel to a distant and exotic land. The second seems to be addressing believers in astrology – "the Zodiac of your life" – whom "a whole new world of gracious living" awaits, and reads like an invitation to consult a good astrologer. In fact, the true answer lies elsewhere. Both are slogans created by developers of large residential complexes situated on the outskirts of Delhi for the benefit of a wealthy clientele in search of a better quality of life.

The language that the developers of these new "chic" residential "colonies" use, the names given them as part of the sales hype, outline the shape that dream cities will take – a blend of ecological utopia and modernist projections, reveal the fantasies, aspirations, and preoccupations of their potential residents, and uncover the constructions of identity accompanying these projects. Yet, it is necessary to compare the projects with the end result, and the promises conjured up by the words with the reality of the urban spaces thus created.

The neighbourhoods that have come up as a result of the residential deconcentration of the privileged to the outskirts of the Indian capital are only one form of spatial expansion highlighting the process of metropolization that is taking place (Dupont, 2000). These high-standing residential estates contrast with other forms of suburban extension such as illegal colonies that are more frequently observed in Third World cities, including Delhi. As it will be shown, the logic of their foundation and *modus vivendi* contribute to an urban pattern based on social segregation and spatial fragmentation, that also reflects a trend common to the process of metropolization in the developing as well as developed world (Davis, 1990; Navez-Bouchanine, 2002).

Dream Towns: the Language of Promoters of Residential Complexes on the Outskirts of Delhi

The evolution of Delhi and its region fits into a proactive town and country planning policy, initiated in the late 1950s. Within the capital itself, this led to the formulation of an urban land policy in 1961 – the scheme for large-scale acquisition, devépment, and disposal of land – and to the elaboration of a Master Plan, executed by the Delhi Development

1
The Delhi Land Finance (DLF) company – a leader in promoting the Dream Towns of a new residential Delhi in the outskirts of earlier Delhis. Photograph: Ruchir Joshi 1999.

2
Tracts of land developed and ready to be built, near Gurgaon. Road traced in an arid landscape. Photograph: Ruchir Joshi 1999.

Authority (the central administration created in 1957). Consequently, all lands within the urbanizable limits of Delhi were placed under the control of this administration, hence creating government monopoly both in land acquisition and supply. The Delhi Development Authority further launched various land development and housing programmes, including the construction of blocks of flats and the allotment of plots to private households or cooperative group housing societies, whereas private builders were excluded from the formal land market. This situation has induced some of the bigger private real estate developers to build residential complexes outside the administrative boundaries of the National Capital Territory, in the neighbouring states of Haryana and Uttar Pradesh. Here building societies can acquire large tracts of land, in keeping with the development plan of the metropolitan area, seeking to favour population deconcentration. The emergence of residential estates in distant rural fringes was allowed by the tremendous increase in private cars,[1] that illustrates the rising of the middle classes in Delhi. These new residential complexes, some in the implementation stage and others still in the project stage, are firstly designed for well-to-do city dwellers, looking for a better life environment. Accordingly, their promoters combine references to nature and modernity in the names chosen for their urban creations and their advertising copy.

Veritable Townships...

These are often presented as independent urban entities, complete with all the requisite amenities and infrastructure. Thus the words *township* and *mini-city* are commonly employed, qualified by adjectives like *self-contained* or *integrated*. To drive home this idea, the word *city* or *town* is added to the name selected for these colonies or residential complexes, as for example: South City, Heritage City, Sentosa City, Malibu Towne, DLF City, etc. The aim of the larger development projects which encompass the whole range of real-estate operations from

Véronique Dupont

constructible plots and individual villas to apartment blocks, is to attain the dimensions of a veritable township. So it is that DLF Qutab Enclave, situated on the outskirts, 23 kilometres from the centre of the capital, boasts of being *Asia's largest private township*. In the Delhi region, it is incontestably the biggest residential complex planned by one single developer (Delhi Land & Finance),[2] covering an area of 1,000 hectares, with a planned housing capacity of 60,000 units, including 46,000 individual houses. The complex will ultimately provide housing for an estimated 2,70,000 residents (DLF, 1993). In comparison, the biggest projects of rival land developers may be likened to "small" townships. For example, Sushant Lok covers an area of 280 hectares, and Sentosa City had planned 152 hectares for building 7,000 dwelling units.

...in the Countryside...

Despite the enormous scale of certain housing projects, the promoters spare no effort to expunge the urban dimension and play down city life by highlighting the rustic/pastoral and ecological/environmental aspects, giving them names reminiscent of natural spaces (Riverdale, Valley View Estate, Spring Fields, Sunbreeze Apartments, Green Meadows, Neelpadm Kunj – blue lotus pond); of greenery (Greenwoods City, Residence Greens, Charmwood Village, Ridgewood Estate); of trees and flowers (Gulmohar Park, Rosewood City, The Palms, Mayfield Gardens, Oakwood Estate); or simply calm and quiet (Sushant Lok – peaceful world, Royal Retreat). Even when the name of the residential complex does not directly evoke nature, this reference is a quasi-constant feature of the publicity and sales spiel handed out by the promoters, with certain recurring key words: *open space, nature, air, green, clean and healthy environment*, in opposition to the words and woes associated with Delhi: pollution, noise, traffic jams. The two biggest real estate developers have thus directly integrated into their slogan or logo expressions such as: *The most environment friendly*

3
Hoarding for Sushant Lok (Ansal Group), "The greenest township south of Delhi", in a particularly arid natural environment.
Photograph: Ruchir Joshi 1999.

township (the DLF group for its Qutab Enclave project) or *The greenest township south of Delhi* (the Ansal group for its Sushant Lok complex). Advertisements combine idyllic images and lyrical expressions in order to touch the environmental sensibility of the urbanites, tired of the pollution and congestion of Delhi. There is no dearth of examples:

. Royal Retreat: *The enchanting burst of profuse greens.... This amazing cluster of natural bounty....* (Eros Group).

. Farmlands: *Dream of a child ... air as pure as nature, trees and gardens, with a thousand birds singing* (Ansal Group).

. Sushant Gardens: *Where life nestles in vast green expanses. Broken only by a beautiful landscaped garden. Bringing with it the long forgotten chirping of birds and humming of bees. Glorious sunshine filtering into your home. Warming your life. Clean, fresh air for healthy, good living* (Ansal Group).

The illustrations, designs, photographs, logos, or even the choice of colours and typeface reinforce the images suggested by the words. The references to ecological and naturalistic utopias were used in a similar manner in the publicity campaigns in Western countries like France of the 1960s and '70s to promote residential projects outside the cities, the new townships and the "new villages" (Brun, 1985).

4
Hoarding in DLF Qutab Enclave,
Phase I: Valley View Estate.
Photograph: Ruchir Joshi 1999.

5
Gateway Tower under construction
in DLF City, Phase III. Photograph:
Ruchir Joshi 1999.

...Modern and Futurist...

The return to nature, "take the cities to the countryside" – as the 19th-century French writer Alphonse Allais had recommended long ago, does not signify the rejection of modernity. Quite the contrary. Modernist and futurist ideology constitutes the second major referent of promotion campaigns of the new suburban residential complexes. Taking advantage of the timing, this tenet in the late '90s was often associated with the metaphor of entry into the third millennium. These references were explicit in slogans such as: *DLF Qutab Enclave – Modern times, Sun City: Metropolis for the next millennium*,[3] or referred to in advertisements:

. At Ansals, we don't just stay in step with the times – we like to stay ahead of the times!
. DLF Qutab Enclave: *It's here. Your opportunity to get into Phase V. The phase of the future!*
. Ardee City: *We have made plans for the next millennium. Have you? Step into the next millennium with an accommodation that is only 15 minutes drive from Indira Gandhi International Airport, New Delhi.*[4]

The modernity argument is also used in the specifications of infrastructure and amenities provided by the developers, often in superlative terms: in DLF Regency Park the infrastructure is *the most modern*, in Rosewood City the commercial complex is *ultra modern*, in Green Meadows the space is *scientifically* planned. As for the business centres that generally come up in the vicinity of new residential districts – as part of integrated township projects and not mere dormitory towns – they are also resolutely turned towards the future: *The Gateway Tower: The place for your future, Millennium Plaza: 21st century corporate park.*

In the context of a developing country like India, the notion of modernity is also implicit in certain geographical referents. First is the reference to the American model, but references to other industrialized or newly industrialized countries, or to international standards, are also highlighted in the descriptions of building and apartment blocks.

6
Abandoned mosque near DLF
Corporate Park, Mehrauli–Gurgaon
Road. Photograph: Ruchir Joshi
1999.

7
Hoarding for Sun City: "Metropolis for the next millennium", in a "future environmental zone coming up", still rather desertlike. Photograph: Ruchir Joshi 1999.

...Imported from the United States, England, and Elsewhere...

The use of foreign toponyms for new housing colonies and residential complexes is frequent: some incorporate names of North American towns and districts (Malibu Towne, Riverdale, Manhattan Apartmansions, Beverly Park, Sun City, Sterling Apartments), English towns (Windsor, Richmond), Canadian (Kingston), Australian (Hamilton Court, Wellington Estate, Clifton Apartments), and even from Singapore (Sentosa City, A mini-Singapore in India). More than a mere geographical referent, often it is also a social referent signifying status and prestige. For the potential buyer who would not have grasped this double referent, the sales talk is generally quite explicit, as the following *advertisements* perfectly illustrate:

. Malibu Condominiums: *American-Style Luxury Apartments.*
. Malibu Towne: *Planned and developed by ex-NRI Californian.*
American suburban ambience. Malibu Towne has been designed to include cul-de-sacs and extensively landscaped to create the ambience of a typical lush green American housing development.
. Sagar Estate's Riverdale: *America – East of Delhi: Citizenship opens today.*
Today we are laying the foundation of a New America, east of Delhi.
The all-America condominium style of life now comes to India....
Riverdale is planned and designed by the Canada-based architect, Ramesh Khosla....
Citizenship is open today to all who like to live in America. ...this condominium captures the spirit of liberty like no other.
Luxury and comfort, till now only seen west of the Atlantic. Now, east of Delhi.

The objective here is to sell the American model as a package, guaranteed, moreover, by the architects who live or have lived in North America; the sort of habitat where everything is American in spirit, atmosphere, type, and style, from the organization of the external spaces and buildings, to the services and equipment provided, the shopping centre, interior design and comfort of the apartments, and even the bathtubs! The builders of these residential complexes *"à l'américaine"* however, have distorted the reference model. Thus the typical lush green terrains found in the Californian city of Malibu, and more generally in Los Angeles, have individual villas with gardens – symbolizing the ideal lifestyle so dear to the Americans (Ghorra-Gobin, 1993) – or small-sized jointly-owned buildings, not more than three storeys high. Much more rare are the fifteen-storey high-rise residential blocks situated in a wooded park, as the model of Malibu Towne shows!
The English style with its old-world charm is also back in fashion:

.Rosewood City: *The luxurious English style township.*
This township will bring back memories of the splendid old world charm of England with scores of bungalows on 115 acres of land.... The club will have distinct British features with a swimming pool, tennis courts and gymnasium for you to relax and unwind.

Such publicity is primarily directed at Non-Resident Indians (NRIs) who want to invest in their home country or are planning to return home one day or another, and who need to be reassured that accommodation and comfort of international standards, such as they are accustomed to, is available in India. This also illustrates how international migration has helped to diffuse architectural standards. Certain housing projects even go to the extent of separating the buildings reserved for the NRIs from the others, thus creating a new form of residential segregation: *Sentosa City will also have exclusive condominium clusters for NRIs with penthouses.* Promoters are able to reach potential clients residing abroad by renting sites on the Internet and participating in international exhibitions.

8 *opposite*
The model of Malibu Towne, newspaper advertisement, January 1995.

Véronique Dupont

MALIBU CONDOMINIUMS
American-Style Luxury Apartments

Planned and developed by ex-NRI Californian

American Suburban Ambience Malibu Towne has been designed to include cul-de-sacs and extensively landscaped to create the ambience of a typical lush green American housing development. With openness and freshness one would love to breathe!

The condominium complex itself has water lagoons, fountains, downs and meadows, and is surrounded by jogging, walking and cycling trails amidst a forest environment.

The condominiums also have uniquely controlled and breathtakingly beautiful surroundings.

Maximum — security colony • Entire colony behind the gates and fully-fenced. • Restricted entry into the colony. • Condominium-complex doubly-secure with world-class security devices, electronic locks and CCTV! • Mobile patrol cars equipped with the latest communications devices and linked with a central communication system.

Facilities • Preferential membership in Malibu Country Club across the road. • American-style shopping complex also across the road. • Nursery, Primary and High Schools within the colony. • Playground for children within the complex itself. • Convenience store within the complex. • Pubs and restaurants. • Theatre actively operational for cultural activities. • Meadows golf club just 2 kms. away. • 'Fireball' disco within 5 minutes drive!

World-Class Design and Conveniences • Entrance lobby is embellished with granite flooring and spectacular atrium! • High-speed super-efficient elevators. • Garbage chutes on each floor • Laundromat in the basement. • Underground parking for each apartment. • Standby generator for all common services. • American-style bathtub and shower sliding glass panels. • Marble in foyer, drawing room, dining room, family-room, kitchen and bathroom; granite counters in bathrooms and kitchen. • Built-in bedroom wardrobes and walk-in closets.

DMS/MT/5

Convenient payment plans

Malibu Plan
□ The Full Payment plan allows an attractive discount
□ The 3-year payment plans is interest-free.

CITI◆HOME
Home loans from Citibank
The 5 to 15 year Citihome Plan make your apartment/property purchase more convenient than ever before!

Govt. approved freehold residential township

Condominium construction started

Call Sales Office: 1001, Ambadeep, 14, Kasturba Gandhi Marg, New Delhi-110 001. Ph.: 3329414, 3721852

Corporate Office: MALIBU HOUSE, 38 DDA, Commercial Complex, Kailash Colony Extension, New Delhi-110 048. Ph.: 6431573, 6419969. Telex: 031-70105 UKPI IN. Fax: 91-11-6447864

Véronique Dupont

...Reserved for an Elite...

Besides the toponyms reminiscent of American or English urban lifestyles, their reputation conferring distinction and status to the residence and thereby to the residents, other names for residential complexes have been selected from words which are symbolic of prestige and elitism. There are names that evoke royalty: Royal Medici, Royal Retreat with its set of apartments The Kings, The Queens, The Princes; others evoke high office: Regency Park with its set of apartments Chancellor, Diplomat, Senator; or precious metals: Platinum, Golden Heights; and luxury sports: Golf Links. The specifications of sites, apartments, infrastructure and services, leisure time activities (exclusive club, swimming pool, tennis courts, golf course, etc.) reinforce the image of luxury, excellence, and class. The epitome of luxury, Hotel Oasis, situated in the vicinity of residential complexes that have come up south of the Territory of Delhi, envisages building a heliport in order to provide a shuttle service for its clients and golfers between the hotel and the international airport! There are also instances when elitism is openly advertised. The publicity brochures of Royal Retreat refer to its *elite residents*, Rosewood City presents itself as an *elitist colony*, and Golf Links as a complex of *residential colonies for the elite*, while Ansals-Anushruti promises *a distinctive neighbourhood of elite homes*, and the promoters of Kant Enclave wax lyrical: *And soon Delhi's most elite neighbourhood will unveil in all its grace. And you the chosen ones will acquire possession of Delhi's most sought after property.*

9 *opposite*
Cowdung cakes drying on a terrace, village enclave in a concrete jungle of high-rise buildings (Chakarpur village). Photograph: Ruchir Joshi 1999.

10
Greenwoods City, newspaper advertisement, March 1999.

...Indian nevertheless?

The names given to the new residential complexes, the slogans and publicity hype of their promoters, are enough to make us forget the geographical and cultural context of their development: Delhi, capital of India! The signs of Indian-ness are rather rare, and in the case of Manhattan Apartmansions they have deliberately been expunged, for its promoters unashamedly proclaim: *The only Indian thing about them is their address*. In the universe of Greenwoods City, the residents shot for publicity photos in joyful familial picnics or outing scenes have definitely abandoned all Indian sartorial habits. Very few names refer to any Hindi or Sanskrit terms: Sushant Lok, Anushruti, Neelpadm Kunj, and Gulmohar Park. A single Indian toponym was noted: Kanchanjunga, after a Himalayan mountain; a sole allusion to one of Delhi's more well-known historical monuments was recorded: DLF Qutab Enclave, referring to the Qutb Minar, the famous minaret built at the end of the 12th century on Delhi's southern periphery, relatively close to the DLF residential complex. The slogans have practically no Hindi words or endogenous cultural references, in fact, only two cases have been identified where promoters have borrowed from the register of "tradition".

The first example is from a hoarding in which the cultural referent to Indian classical music has been combined with a rustic image: *Morning Raga at DLF* is illustrated by the picture of a cock crowing. The second, an advertisement spread over two whole pages of a national daily, is a remarkable blend of references to the modern cosmopolitan city with endogenous architectural traditions. Sentosa City firstly projects itself as a "mini-Singapore in India", a futurist city illustrated by the picture of a group of brilliantly lit skyscrapers,

11
Sentosa City, doublespread newspaper advertisement, December 1996.

Véronique Dupont

conceived according to international standards and equipped with the most modern facilities. But this city of the future also advertises itself as the *Zodiac of your life*, built according to the *vastu* principles, as set down in this ancient science on architecture:

> *Vastu approved: The entire city is conceived on the auspicious circle of the zodiac, and appropriately its residential condominiums are named after the various signs of the zodiac. Residents of each condominium are assured of protection against all evils by the star it is named after. Our cosmic consultant Mr Rajesh Rya made a critical "vastu" assessment and ensured that lady luck smiles on its residents from the moment they step into Sentosa City.*

The first group of buildings in the new city is thus named *Sentosa Capricorn:*

> . Sentosa Capricorn: *Born today under the sign of the Capricorn we have proved an ancient science right.*
> *The 10th sign of the Zodiac Capricorn stands for power and authority, brilliance and innovation, makes rapid headway and assures success. Sentosa Capricorn is perfectly positioned to achieve this.*

The finality of the message could also be the conclusion of its content analysis: *Reality beyond imagination.* [5]

A careful reading of the sales pitch also reveals other signs of the Indian city, not the traditional city but the metro city of today, with its everyday problems: *24 hour water and power supply.* Could this ever be used as a sales gambit in the European or American urban context? Probably not, such trivial commodities would not be considered worth mentioning in an advertisement, and even less so where posh residential complexes are concerned. On the other hand, constant electricity cuts and water shortage, that are a serious handicap for Delhi's residents, make the regular and guaranteed supply of these two basic services a rare luxury, necessitating their mention in a publicity brochure. As for details on the caretaking facilities offered, they highlight the growing security phobia of Delhi's well-to-do citizens. This is a concern common to other large metropolises of the world, and reflects the glaring inequalities in the economic conditions and habitats of the different sections of urban society.

12
DLF City Phase V: hoarding on the Mehrauli–Gurgaon Road, near Sikandapur village. Photograph: Ruchir Joshi 1999.

13
On the left-hand side of the wall,
nature reconstituted: a park
landscaped in DLF Qutab Enclave
Phase III. On the right-hand side,
the adjoining village of Nathupur:
fallow land in its natural condition.
Photograph: Ruchir Joshi 1999.

The proximity of the Indira Gandhi International Airport, a factor which is systematically emphasized by promoters of all new residential complexes situated on the rural fringes south of the Territory of Delhi, is also a reminder of the geographic context. But this reminder is ambiguous: is it a simple indicator of location? or is the message also meant to convey the international dimension, an easily accessible gateway to foreign countries?

From the Project Stage to the Realization Stage: a Disillusioned Lot of Residents

Do these new high-class neighbourhoods, these futurist and ecological residential complexes, fulfil the promises made in the advertisements? Does reality conform to the dreams conjured by the words?

A simple visit to the rural fringes undergoing urbanization in south Delhi, where many of the residential complexes are to be found, is sufficient to sow some doubt. The parks and green areas marked in the site plan are an essential component of the proposed lifestyle, the ecological and environmental alternatives advanced by the promoters, whereas the natural environment here is arid, the vegetation very poor with vast stretches of denuded land; no oaks (a species in any case alien to the local plant habitat), no palm trees, no hawthorn bushes, no forests, no lush green prairies.... As for the parks and plantations laid out by the developers, they are very unequally developed depending on the different residential complexes and the age of the plantation; in certain zones, the tree cover is at best very sparse.

To listen to the residents' complaints on these new satellite townships, through interviews conducted in the DLF Qutab Enclave or from shared experiences in newspaper articles, it seems that the utilities and services announced are often still inadequate and at times even absent several years after the first residents moved in. In other residential complexes, all the promised hallmarks of elegance and luxury have remained on paper. The poor quality of the finish in no way corresponds to the proclaimed international norms, and no vegetation worth the name greens the outer areas of the buildings.

Attractive hoardings, enticing advertisements, exaggerated language...a complete dupe: classic violations and sales strategies that mark publicity campaigns the world over! The question is whether the sales talk should be interpreted as a straightforward publicity gambit, or also as an answer to the real needs and desires of urbanites.

In this context, the example of DLF Qutab Enclave has many lessons to offer. As shown by the investigation conducted in this vast residential complex, property ownership is the principal motive quoted by the inhabitants to explain their change of domicile within the metropolitan area of Delhi. For these new property owners, the choice of residence is firstly a matter of financial consideration, the cost of plots or dwelling units being more affordable here than in the capital, where the shortage of constructible land for development is acute. In particular, despite the inflationary prices of land and housing in DLF Qutab Enclave, the prices are definitely lower than those commanded in south Delhi, a zone much sought after by the rich because of the social status that it confers on its residents. The prestige and status attached to the new residential complexes render them an attractive alternative for the middle and upper classes.

However, the environmental considerations advanced by promoters in their publicity campaigns are also present. Thus the search for a better quality of life and more space are reasons often cited by the residents, particularly amongst those who had lived in Delhi earlier (and represent a large majority group). No doubt, this new localization means longer distances to the work place but this inconvenience is compensated for by the prospect of a more peaceful and less polluted environment than if they lived in the city proper. For those who were already owners of a house or an apartment in the capital, these comparative advantages constitute the principal reason for the new acquisition. The environmental factor can also be a major consideration for the richer, who can afford to invest in real estate in south Delhi, but choose to settle in DLF Qutab Enclave, which they believe offers a better quality of life. In addition, the environmental factor has played a crucial role in families deciding to leave Delhi and settle permanently in the new locality. Despite complaints about the inadequate utilities and services in their present residential complex, they in no way envisage returning to a more central – but perforce a more congested – part of the capital.

14
Luxurious villas in DLF Qutab Enclave Phase I, on Gurgaon-Faridabad Marg. Photograph: Surendra S. Rajan 1995.

15
Façade of luxurious villas in
DLF Qutab Enclave Phase II.
Photograph: Ruchir Joshi 1999.

If economic reasons predominate in the choice of a decentralized residence, environmental awareness and considerations of status are also present. These themes, fully exploited in promotional campaigns, seem also to correspond to the expectations of well-off urbanites, tired of an alienating urban environment.

Conclusion

The vocabulary of the private promoters, with their very positivist and ambitious tone, their symbolic and evocative names and lyrical descriptions, project the new residential complexes as fully independent and modern urban entities, yet in a bucolic environment. Environmental referents, the "hygienist" utopias (clean air and nature), are part of quasi-universal recurrent arguments, lauding the merits of urban decentralization. References to modernity – implicitly conveying that this modernity is not obvious in the geo-cultural context in question, and, in a related register, the reference to the American model, seem more specific to the context of a developing country. The large Indian community residing abroad, especially in the United States, constituting a potential clientele for real-estate investments in the home country, probably inspires promoters of residential complexes on the outskirts of the Indian capital to multiply the symbols of a habitat and lifestyle imported from the West.[6]

Identity-related constructions concurrent with the promotion of these residential projects for the well-to-do also reflect a phenomenon of greater socio-spatial fragmentation. The search for selectivity and elitism, conveyed by these names, the descriptions and sales hype so typical of this trade, reflect the glaring divide between rich and poor in the great metropolises of the Third World, and reinforce a tendency towards ghettoization with the former seeking to "protect themselves" from the latter.

ACKNOWLEDGEMENT

This text is partially based on my paper written in French, "Les nouveaux quartiers chics de Delhi. Langage publicitaire et réalités périurbaines", in H. Rivière d'Arc (ed.), *Nommer les nouveaux territoires urbains*, Paris, UNESCO/Maison des Sciences de l'Homme, 2001, pp. 39–61.

Véronique Dupont

NOTES

1.   In 1995, the number of registered cars in Delhi reached 5,75,762, which was more than the aggregated number of registered cars in Mumbai, Kolkata, and Chennai altogether (source of data: *Motor Transport Statistics of India*, 1996, Transport Research Wing, Ministry of Surface Transport, Government of India, New Delhi).

2.   DLF had already been a prime land developer of Delhi in the 1950s, with several residential colonies to its credit, including Model Town, Greater Kailash, South Extension, etc.

3.   Slogan recorded in 1999.

4.   Slogan recorded in 1999.

5.   Eventually, the heavily advertised Sentosa City project did not come up, as the Ghaziabad Development Authority cancelled the agreement with the project's developer in 1997.

6.   As part of his research project on "The spaces of transnational cultures", A. King (2002) shows that, although "the international advertising and marketing of substantial 'Western-style' suburban residential property has…increasingly become a form of globalized practice", the existence of a large NRI diaspora "gives the new suburban phenomenon [around Indian metropolitan cities]…distinctive characteristics"; in particular "it helps to explain the culturally distinctive visual, spatial, typological, architectural, and naming practices of new suburban development" (pp. 79–80).

SOURCES OF INFORMATION AND DATA

Advertisements in the Delhi edition of the mainline English dailies (mostly *The Times of India* and *The Pioneer*) from end-1993 to mid-1998 as well as press reviews, with partial updating till 2002.

Publicity hoardings observed in the Delhi region from end-1993 to mid-1998 with a renewed visit in March–April 1999.

Publicity brochures prepared by the promoters for distribution to potential buyers, as well as their official reports.

Websites of four major real estate developers operating in the Delhi region (Eros Group, Delhi Land Finance, Ansals, Mittals Property), each group presenting a number of its development operations and projects.

This writer's migration survey conducted in DLF Qutab Enclave in 1995, covering a representative sample of 164 households, completed with in-depth interviews by Mriga Sidhu in 1997.

REFERENCES

Brun, J., 1985. "Nouvelles approches", in G. Duby (ed.), *Histoire de la France urbaine*, Volume 5: *La ville aujourd'hui*. Paris, Seuil, pp. 333–91.

Davis, M., 1990. *City of Quartz: Excavating the Future in Los Angeles*. London, Verso.

Dupont, V., 2000. "Spatial and demographic growth of Delhi and the main migration flows", in V. Dupont, E. Tarlo, D. Vidal (eds.), *Delhi. Urban Space and Human Destinies*. Delhi, Manohar/Centre de Sciences Humaines, pp. 229–39.

DLF Universal Ltd., 1993. "Environmental appraisal of a new town. DLF Qutab Enclave, Haryana (A residential complex)". Submitted to Ministry of Environment and Forests, Government of India by DLF Universal Ltd., New Delhi.

Ghorra-Gobin, C., 1993. *Les Etats Unis, espace, environnement, société, ville*. Paris, Nathan.

King, Anthony D., 2002. "Speaking from the margins: 'Postmodernism,' transnationalism, and the imagining of contemporary Indian urbanity", in R. Grant and J. Rennie (eds.), *Globalization and the Margins*. Basingstoke and New York, Palgrave Macmillan, pp. 72–90.

Navez-Bouchanine, F. (ed.), 2002. *La fragmentation en question. Des villes entre fragmentation spatiale et fragmentation sociale?* Paris, L' Harmattan.

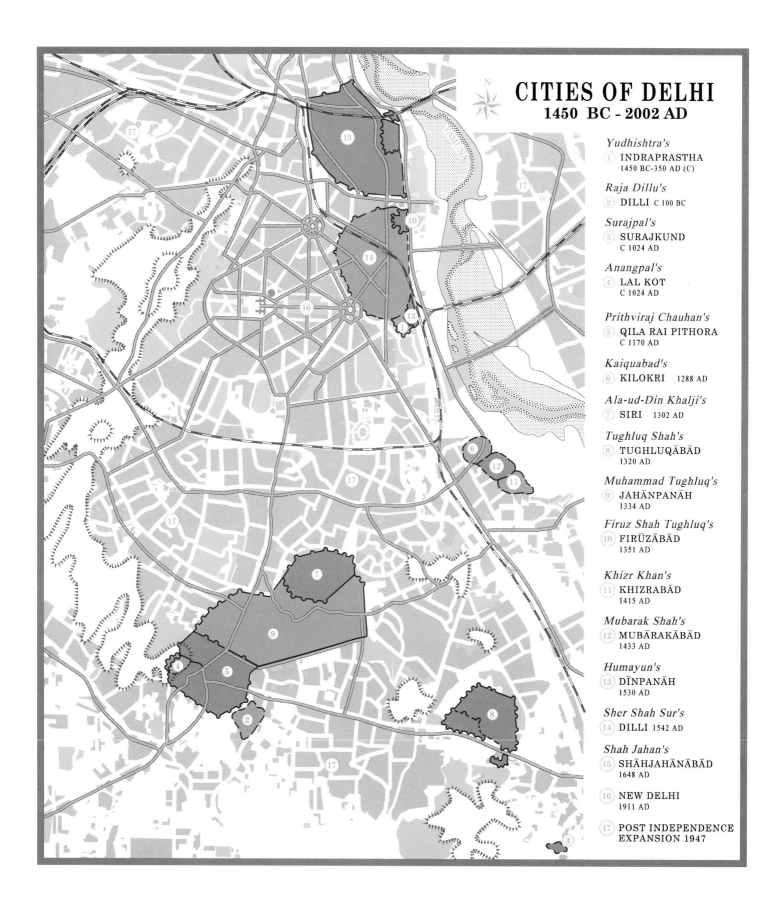

CITIES OF DELHI
1450 BC - 2002 AD

Yudhishtra's
① INDRAPRASTHA
1450 BC-350 AD (C)

Raja Dillu's
② DILLI C 100 BC

Surajpal's
③ SURAJKUND
C 1024 AD

Anangpal's
④ LAL KOT
C 1024 AD

Prithviraj Chauhan's
⑤ QILA RAI PITHORA
C 1170 AD

Kaiquabad's
⑥ KILOKRI   1288 AD

Ala-ud-Din Khalji's
⑦ SIRI   1302 AD

Tughluq Shah's
⑧ TUGHLUQĀBĀD
1320 AD

Muhammad Tughluq's
⑨ JAHĀNPANĀH
1334 AD

Firuz Shah Tughluq's
⑩ FIRŪZĀBĀD
1351 AD

Khizr Khan's
⑪ KHIZRABĀD
1415 AD

Mubarak Shah's
⑫ MUBĀRAKĀBĀD
1433 AD

Humayun's
⑬ DĪNPANĀH
1530 AD

Sher Shah Sur's
⑭ DILLI 1542 AD

Shah Jahan's
⑮ SHĀHJAHĀNĀBĀD
1648 AD

⑯ NEW DELHI
1911 AD

⑰ POST INDEPENDENCE
EXPANSION 1947

S.M. Chadha

S.M. Chadha

Mapping Delhi

Here we stand in Delhi city, symbol of old India and the new. It is not the narrow lanes and houses of old Delhi or wide spaces and rather pretentious buildings of New Delhi that count, but the spirit of this ancient city. For Delhi has been an epitome of India's history with its succession of glory and disaster, and with its great capacity to absorb many cultures and yet remain itself. It is a gem with many facets, some bright and some darkened by age, presenting the course of India's life and thought during the ages. Even the stones here whisper to our ears of the ages of long ago and the air we breathe is full of the dust and fragrance of the past, as also of the fresh and piercing winds of the present. We face the good and bad of India in Delhi city which has been the grave of many empires and the nursery of a republic. What a tremendous story is here; the tradition of millennia of our history surrounds us at every step, and the procession of innumerable generations passes by before our eyes....

– Jawaharlal Nehru

In September 1992 I received a call from Vikram Lal of Eicher. I did not know him but Eicher sounded familiar as the company that makes tractors. Lal, a keen map aficionado, wanted to make a map of Delhi. He asked me whether I would undertake this task. To me this was a dream come true. The creation of maps and mapping were in my blood. After retirement from the Survey of India, I had always wanted to make a detailed map of Delhi, but due to lack of resources needed for such a large venture, I had been unable to do so. So you can imagine my happiness and excitement, as I accepted Lal's offer of doing what I most wanted to do.

This great city, Delhi, the capital of our country, has a long and chequered history. The city we see at present is a mishmash of many upheavals and circumstances which the region underwent. But first let us have an overview of its topography and how the city grew to become one of the greatest and oldest capital cities of the world.

Delhi – Older than the Himalaya

Delhi is believed to be ten times older than even the Himalaya. This region came into existence 1,000 million years ago, but remained submerged for about 400 million years. It reappeared during the Great Convulsion around 600 million years ago, while the Himalaya arose about 500 million years later. The sea which had washed the Delhi Ridge subsequently disappeared. If the entire span of geological history is taken as 24 hours, the period of human settlement in the Delhi Triangle, since the founding of the legendary city of Indraprastha, is represented by 4/60th of a second!

1 *opposite*
The historic cities of Delhi. Its various rulers established a series of citadels in the Aravalli hills and on the banks of the Yamuna.

The Delhi Triangle

The abundant Yamuna river along with the Northern, Central, and Southern Ridges (the trailing ends of the Aravalli Hills), formed the Delhi triangle which enclosed an area of roughly 180 square kilometres. The area around the Yamuna was low-lying, sandy, and prone to floods. The Northern and Central Ridges were covered with dense forest that reached down to the Yamuna. The ridges were thick and impenetrable and inhabited by wild animals. The rocky Southern Ridge was desolate and almost barren. Many streams emanating from the ridges fed the triangle and flowed into the Yamuna. This triangle, with natural fortifications on all sides and located at the centre of northern India, became the choice of kings for their capital cities. It was also strategically located on the great northern highway linking Pataliputra (Patna) with Taxila (near Rawalpindi). Buddhist monks took this route on their journey to Central Asia as did invaders from the northwest.

Delhi became the gateway to India.

Each group of invaders plundered the city of its wealth only to rebuild it as their own capital though at a different site. Different groups chose different sites but remained within this triangular haven.

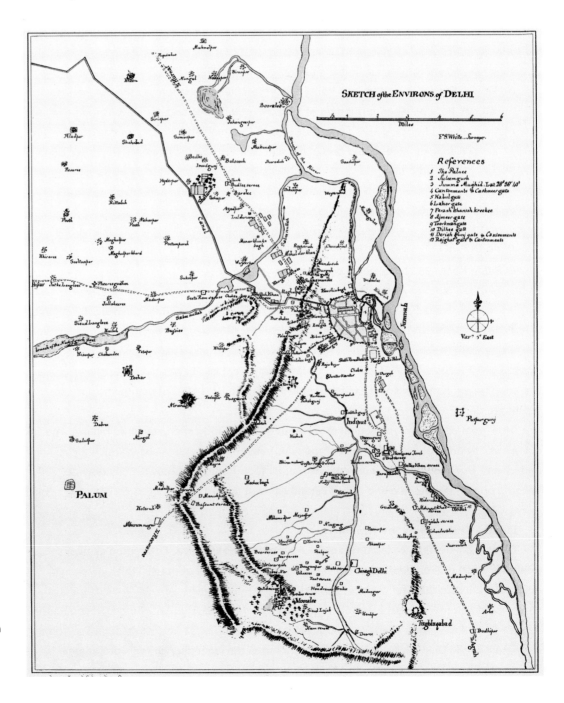

2
Until very recently the cities of Delhi were founded within the triangular territory defined by the hills and the river. This 1807 sketch of Delhi was reproduced in a souvenir titled "Survey of India through the Ages".

S.M. Chadha

The Many Cities of Delhi

The legendary Pandavas (circa 1450 BCE) are said to have founded the earliest known capital city of Indraprastha. Maya, the architect built a splendid palace and court for them. The *Mahabharata* describes how the forest was set on fire and the ground levelled for the city to be built on the west bank of the Yamuna. It flourished for eighteen centuries before fading into the mists of legend.

There are various views as to how Delhi derived its name. It may have come from Raja Dillu's Dilli (circa 100 BCE), which was sited about 10 kilometres southwest of Indraprastha.

The next big city to emerge was Surajkund (circa 1024 CE) established by the Tomaras, about 7 kilometres southeast of Dilli on the Southern Ridge. The large amphitheatre reservoir built by them is today a popular resort and picnic spot.

In 1024, Anangapal of the Tomaras, shifted the city 11 kilometres to the northwest on a rocky outcrop of the Southern Ridge. Some ramparts of this fine walled city called Lal Kot are extant.

In 1170, the Rajput king famous for his chivalry, Prithviraja Chauhan, also known as Rai Pithora, expanded the city four times, built fine temples, and also a tall tower. The city was enclosed by high walls and came to be known as Qila Rai Pithora.

The Turks overthrew the Rajputs and usurped Qila Rai Pithora as their capital city in the early 13th century. The first nine Muslim kings ruled from here. During the time 27 Hindu and Jain temples were apparently pulled down to build the Quwwat-ul-Islam. The big tower was converted into the Qutb Minar. After about a century Kaiqubad shifted the capital once again, to Kilokri in 1288, about 10 kilometres northwest, on the lower western bank of the Yamuna. It is said the river reduced it to rubble.

In 1302, Siri was built by the famous and ambitious Alaudin Khalji, just over 2 kilometres from Lal Kot. The city lay within a circular fort with seven gates outside which was dug a large reservoir, Hauz Khas, for its people.

Tughluq Shah built his capital Tughluqabad in 1320, about 5 kilometres southeast of Siri, on the barren Southern Ridge. However, his successor, Muhammad Tughluq built his new capital Jahanpanah in 1334, between Siri and Qila Rai Pithora. And in 1351, Firuzshah Tughluq built his capital about 10 kilometres north-northeast of Siri and called it Firuzabad (presently Ferozshah Kotla). It covered a large area, spreading like a fan from the citadel.

The triangle lay dormant for a century and a half when the Lodis transferred their capital to Agra. Then in 1530, Humayun laid the foundations of a new capital Dinpanah, on the old site of Indraprastha. It was expanded and completed by Sher Shah Suri in 1542 and called Dilli. The king built big strong walls around it as seen in the Purana Qila.

The next Mughals, Akbar and Jahangir, shifted their capitals outside Delhi, but Akbar's grandson, Shahjahan, built a grand city on

3
Delhi and its environs, archival map, pre-Independence.

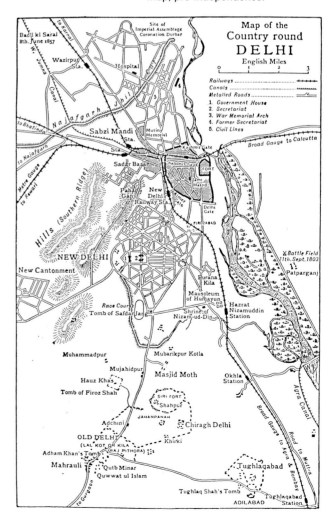

Shāhjahānābād

DELHI around 1850

Redrawn, by courtesy of the British Library, Oriental and India Office Collections.

from an original manuscript in the India Office Records. Archive reference: India Office Records X/1659

Printed with financial support by Deutsche Forschungsgemeinschaft (DFG)

Editors: E. Ehlers, Th. Krafft, J. Malik

Design and Cartography: G. Storbeck

Printing: Landesvermessungsamt Nordrhein-Westfalen

© Geographische Institute der Universität Bonn 1992

4
A redrawn map of Shahjahanabad derived from an 1850 hand-drawn map in the Oriental and India Office Collections. Source: *Shahjahanabad/Old Delhi,* eds. Eckart Ehlers, Thomas Krafft, and J. Malik, Franz Steiner Verlag, Stuttgart, 1992, copyright Geographische Institute der Universitat Bonn.

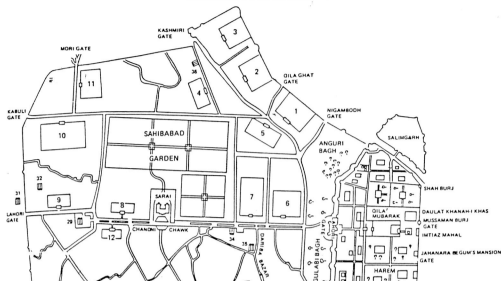

SHAHJAHANABAD: 1739

5

Shahjahanabad, 1739.
Detail showing eight of the gates,
and the gardens. From Stephen P.
Blake, *Shahjahanabad*, New Delhi,
1993.

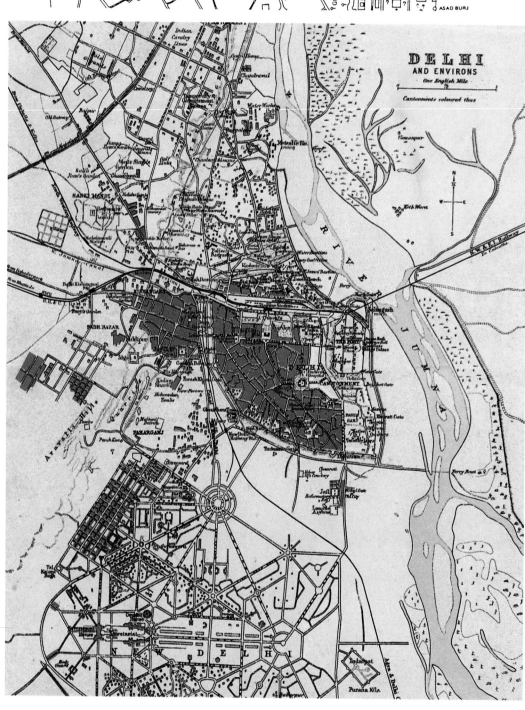

6

Map from the *Imperial Gazetteer
Atlas of India*, 1931.

S.M. Chadha

the banks of the Yamuna. It had well laid out parks, gardens, *katra*s, *kucha*s, and the famous Chandni Chowk, once said to be the richest street in the world. Through this street ran a channel to water horses and camels which came laden with merchandise. He called this city Shahjahanabad and moved here from Agra in 1648 on completion of the palaces within the impressive and formidable Lal Qila. The city fort walls were over 6 kilometres in length, had 27 towers with 14 gates, many of which still exist. It was from this city that the Mughal emperors reached the zenith of their power and magnificence. Today this part is called Purani Dilli, the erstwhile commercial hub of Delhi. The very interesting 1739 map shows the 14 gates, gardens, havelis, and all the other features of this grand city.

Delhi had acquired a mystic aura; it engendered the belief that he who holds Delhi rules India.

In 1931 the British shifted their capital from Calcutta to the planned garden city of Lutyens' and Baker's majestic New Delhi, with its well laid-out avenues and circles. It lay south of Shahjahanabad and covered about 26 square kilometres.

In 1947 with Independence came an influx of five lakh refugees from Pakistan. They were settled in rehabilitation colonies in Jangpura, Nizamuddin, and Lajpat Nagar, just south of Delhi and some even across the Ridge in Rajendra Nagar, Karol Bagh, and Patel Nagar.

Delhi in the 21st century continues to grow, engulfing all the ancient and modern city sites. Today from about 6 1/2 square kilometres covered by Shahjahanabad and 26 square kilometres comprising Lutyens' New Delhi, it has spread to about 750 square kilometres crossing the Yamuna and over the Northern, Central, and Southern Ridges. If you consider the contiguous urban sprawl of Gurgaon, NOIDA, Faridabad, and Ghaziabad, it covers over 1,200 square kilometres!

Eighty years ago, Delhi's population was probably not more than two lakhs. It increased to about seven times that number when India became a republic in 1950. And today a steadily increasing population of over 138.5 lakhs inhabits the city.

The heterogeneous background of this great city meant mapping it was always a big challenge.

The Survey of India

The Survey of India (SOI) was established in 1767 and is the oldest scientific department of the Government of India.

The early history of the SOI followed the East India Company's expanding areas of influence and conquest. It started with the Presidencies of Bengal, Bombay, and Madras and inched its way across the length and breadth of India, including that of Delhi. The Surveyor General was stationed in Calcutta and his headquarters moved to Delhi only in 1940, that too for a short period, before moving up to Mussoorie and then down to Dehra Dun.

Surveys and mapping involve two basic elements: the measurement of angles and of distances. When establishing a control network, i.e. determination of the latitude, longitude, and height of points on the earth's surface, these elements are measured with the greatest precision.

Up to the 18th century surveys were piecemeal and not based on a rigid control network. In hostile territory route surveys were undertaken. Maps were hand drawn, and mostly in single colour. Traces were made and distributed.

George Everest, Surveyor General of India 1830–43, put the Survey of India and India on the map of the world.

The 2,400 kilometre Great Meridonial Arc initiated by Lambton in 1802, was completed by George Everest in 1841 – it started from Cape Comorin and ended at the foothills of the Himalaya. Delhi lay en route of this massive expedition. This determined the shape and size of the earth, and is called the Everest Spheroid. This best fits the shape of the earth's gravity equi-potential surface for India and adjacent countries. All mathematical calculations in the Indian subcontinent are based till today on the Everest Spheroid.

During the period 1800 to 1843, compilation of topographical surveys based on route surveys was gradually discarded and surveys based on geodetic control commenced. Delhi was no exception.

In the early part of the 20th century there were complaints from military authorities that SOI maps were not "modern". In 1905 a high-level committee formulated a policy and programme to meet military and survey needs. Survey methods and map-making techniques were standardized and contoured multicolour maps were introduced. A system to cover the entire subcontinent was evolved. These form till today, the basis of all mapping within this region.

Measuring Angles

Theodolites are used for measuring angles between points a few kilometres to over 80 kilometres apart. For longer rays they have to be positioned on vantage points, the higher the better. Older theodolites were heavy and bulky. Transporting them through jungles, up tall buildings, towers and on to hilltops, posed a lot of problems. The Great Theodolite used by George Everest weighed 459 kilograms when packed. It was fitted with a 36 inch horizontal circle with 5 verniers and an 18 inch vertical circle. Today, theodolites of even better precision weigh no more than a few kilograms.

To get good readings, observation lines to predetermined points have to be cleared of jungle and the weather has to be fine; cloudy days made surveyors spend many a night on hilltops. After the control points are established and coordinates determined, they are plotted on a drawing sheet which is mounted on a plane table (a flat top instrument mounted on a folding tripod). The plane table is positioned at well-distributed vantage points and the ground details are surveyed with a sight rule. The general accuracy is maintained by the principle of "working from the whole to the part". The whole being the geodetic control network.

Colonel George Everest, along with his erstwhile assistant Joseph Olliver carried out the work and observations of the Great Meridonial Arc, and established control points around Delhi between 1832–35. As the plains were dead flat, around fourteen towers were constructed for the purpose of theodolite observations. The team had difficulty in clearing long lines of sight as the plain was covered with towns, villages, and tree clusters. The Yamuna valley was dead flat. Everest reports that Olliver had trouble to the south of Delhi as robberies and murders committed thereabouts were so widespread that they caused panic among his followers and rendered it impossible for him to proceed with his project.

An objection frequently raised against the occupation of high buildings as points of observation, was that the privacy of women's quarters might be infringed upon. Though these scruples had to be respected Everest could not resist mocking at the request of a wealthy householder that the surveyor should withdraw to a less convenient situation where he could build a tower to any height he liked. The cost of the move and the tower would be paid for by the zamindar.

Another point of concern among the local people was that the telescopes had magical powers which could invert and turn women upside down – an indecent posture no doubt and very shocking to contemplate. But the arduous Great Trigonometrical Survey passed through Delhi towards the Himalaya, leaving no time for such speculative amusement.

The SOI made India one of the best-mapped countries of the world.

Revenue Surveys

Geographical maps were not found suitable for the administration of land, its extent and nature, and for the collection of revenue. The Revenue Surveys by the SOI began from Bengal. The Revenue Surveys of Delhi were initiated in 1822 by Thomas Oliver and were revised in

7
Survey of India Delhi Guide Map, surveyed 1984.

S.M. Chadha

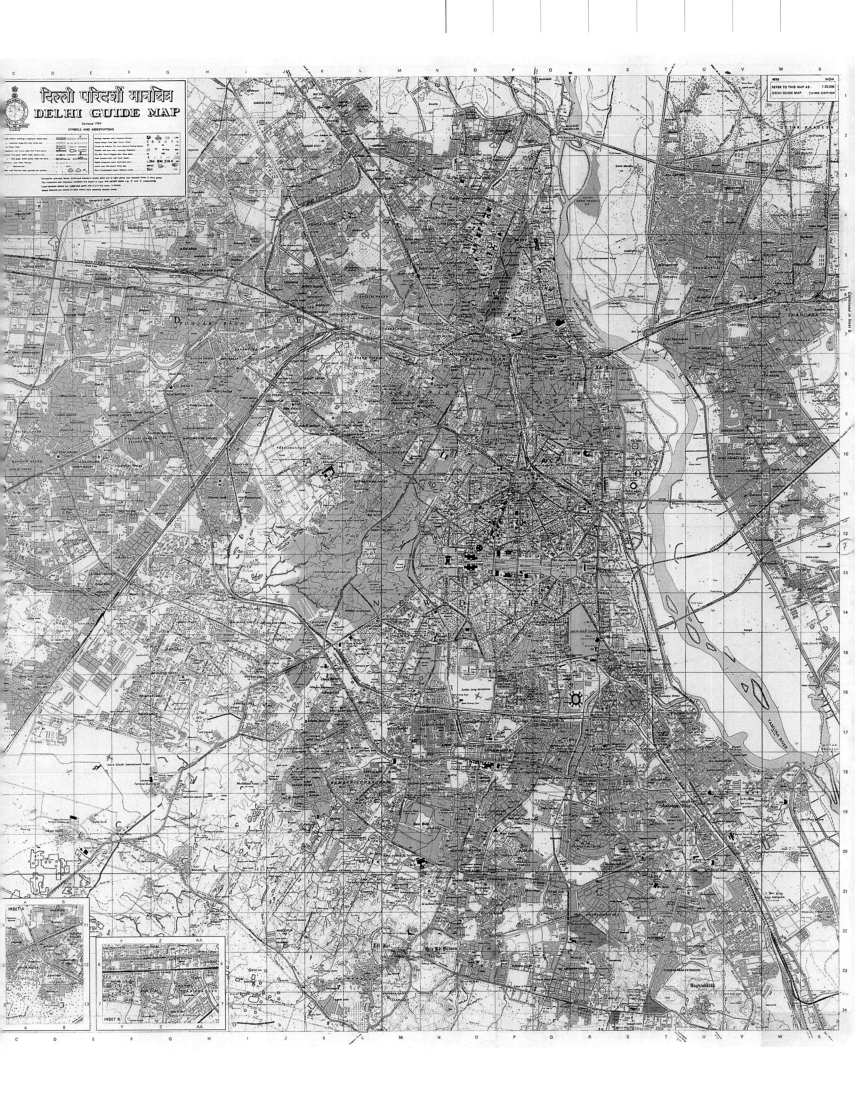

1870–72. The territories of Delhi at that time included Ambala, Hissar, Ludhiana, and Ferozepore.

The 1905 Survey Committee, which formulated SOI's policy and programme to meet military needs, transferred revenue surveys from the SOI and made them the responsibility of the provinces.

Some Interesting Maps and Surveys

Forerunners of the army and sometimes in its wake, surveyors had the onerous task of exploring the unknown. As the British marched west, new districts beyond the Yamuna were entrusted to Francis White. This British surveyor had been surveying the marches of Colonel Ball's brigade beyond Rewari during 1805–06, and prepared a map of the country lying within the "Triangle of Dilee, Hawsee and Jaypoor". He surveyed the "Sketch of the Environs of Delhi" in the year 1807. Its hand-drawn original is with the Survey of India, Dehra Dun. It is an interesting map showing many villages and locations which are familiar even today such as Talkatora, Ricabganj, Janturmantur, Chiragh Delhi, Mooralee (Mehrauli) etc. But the main town is that of Shahjahanabad. It gives the accurate latitude of Jama Masjid – 28 degrees 38 minutes 40 seconds. This was surveyed on a scale of 0.79 inch to a mile. Interestingly a canal coming into the city of Shahjahanabad from the northwest is also shown on the map.

Another interesting map of Shahjahanabad, on a large scale, was made around the year 1850. It shows nearly all the *gali*s and *kucha*s and large gardens north of Chandni Chowk, now obliterated and occupied by Old Delhi Railway Station.

Mention must also be made of the 1912 Delhi map, which was specially prepared by the SOI for the Home Department, based on the Delhi surveys and the Home Revenue surveys of 1870–72. It was on this map that the proposed layout of New Delhi was presented to the government in 1913.

As mentioned earlier, the 1905 Committee laid down modern standards to produce multicoloured contoured maps. Delhi and its surrounding areas were first surveyed by the SOI on these modern lines on a scale of one inch to a mile in the year 1912.

In 1967, India adopted the metric system of weights and measures. The SOI therefore went metric and maps covering Delhi were resurveyed on a scale 1:50,000 between 1975 and 1977.

The Eicher City Map

Coming back to my conversation with Vikram Lal who expressed a desire to give Delhi a world-class map: After some discussions it became clear that the map should cover the whole contiguous urban sprawl, therefore the satellite towns of Gurgaon, Ghaziabad, Faridabad, and NOIDA were also included. It had to be up-to-date, satisfy customer needs, and be user-friendly. The guiding principle would be to help a person reach within 20–30 metres of his destination. This was of course very tough for, unlike other cities of the world, most of Delhi's roads within colonies are not named. To overcome this problem it was decided that not only colony and road names but also block numbers and house numbers needed to be shown.

In my 33 years of surveying and mapping with the SOI, this was the first time that I had the freedom to create my own map design – i.e. information content, layout, style, colours, hues, symbols, and methodology. Yes, for once I was not tied down by the hundred-year-old map specifications of the SOI. It was a great feeling.

The best source for extracting the most current infrastructure – roads and railway lines, built-up areas, land use, etc. – is aerial photography. But in India aerial photography is classified as "top secret". So we decided to go in for the next best alternative i.e. high-resolution satellite imagery. Luckily at that time we could obtain French SPOT Imagery.

We decided to augment this with colony layout plans. This we discovered to our dismay, was a Herculean task. It transpired that some authorities were afraid to give us the layout

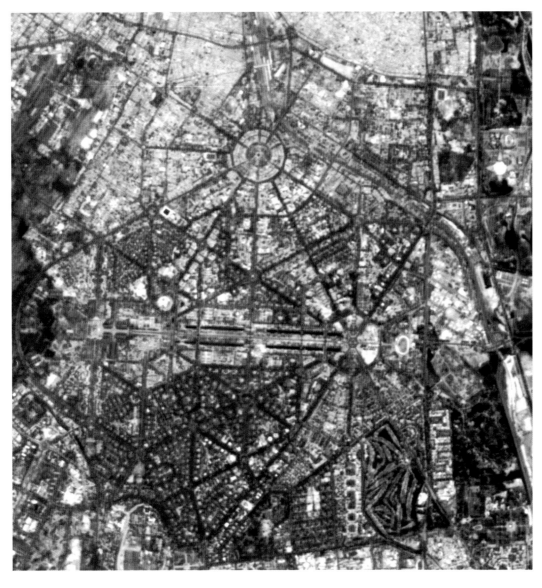

8
Satellite image of Delhi city.

plans, lest some persons owning property take them to court; others just did not want to share them with us. Eventually we managed to collect over 800 locality layout plans. But it took much time and effort.

Compilation

From the satellite imagery we captured the limits of the contiguous urban sprawl to be mapped. Then the area was divided into map pages. We decided upon a scale of 1:12,500 as we found it optimal to accommodate the rich information content we had planned, which included house numbers.

The map was compiled on computers using the latest mapping software and we generated a digital cartographic database. We obtained geocoded satellite imagery. Roads, lanes, and other limits that were clearly visible on the satellite image were used as the control network. The layout plans were on different scales and most of them were not very accurate. These were properly scaled and warped to the control network provided by the geocoded satellite imagery. Thereafter the maps were digitized. Pagewise maps were extracted and plotted on a scale 1:10,000 on thick drawing paper for field verification surveys.

Field Surveys

The whole area was systematically and comprehensively ground surveyed, computer plots were corrected and updated, and the required information and details captured. This was done in six layers. It was a difficult and tedious task. Slowly and steadily the work progressed.

Inch by inch the fabric of Delhi was woven. Areas varied from the well ordered Lutyens' New Delhi to the congested and crowded commercial areas of Karol Bagh and Old Delhi, and the haphazard cramped unauthorized colonies. Surveying Shahjahanabad was very difficult, some surveyors even lost their way in its narrow *gali*s. We had to be very careful with names and their categories as picked by the surveyors. For example, one surveyor put Archie's Gallery (a shop) under Art Galleries and another designated one-or-two bed clinics as hospitals! Regular field inspections and examination of records and maps were carried out to ensure purity of data.

Computerization, Processing, and Printing

All the field data received were fed into computers and the residing digital data corrected and updated. Map pages were plotted and thoroughly examined. Mistakes had to be carefully located and corrected.

Our maps were generated on PCs whereas the printing industry works on MACs. These two systems did not see eye to eye. In those days software was stand-alone. I suppose this was to dissuade users going in for another firm's software. Transfer of data and processing it to generate four-colour positives also became a very big problem. We searched for translators in India and abroad but to no avail. Then we tried out conventional methodology, but it did not give us the desired standard of printing. After many months the company which had supplied

9
Eicher map of Delhi today.

10 *opposite*
Part of the Eicher map showing central Delhi.

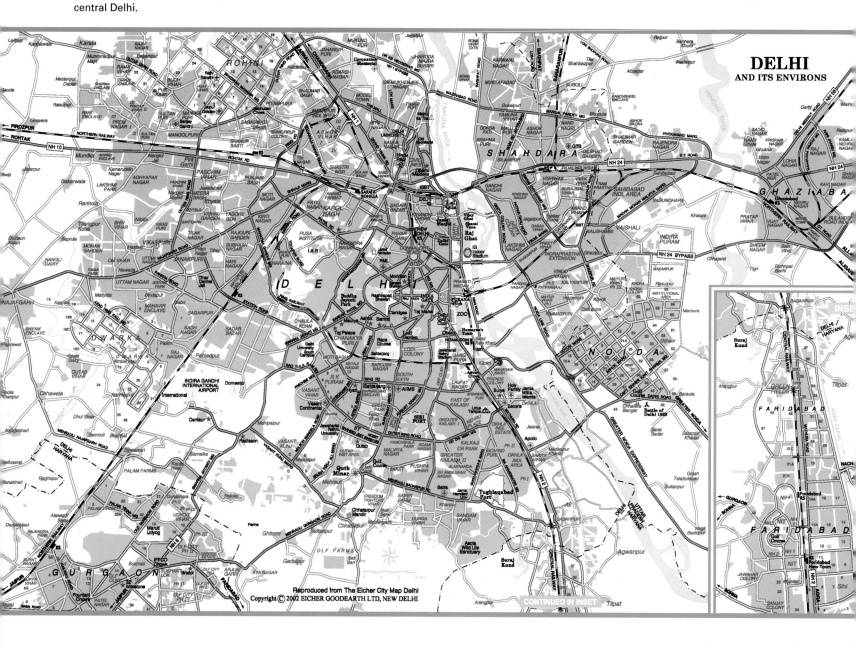

S.M. Chadha

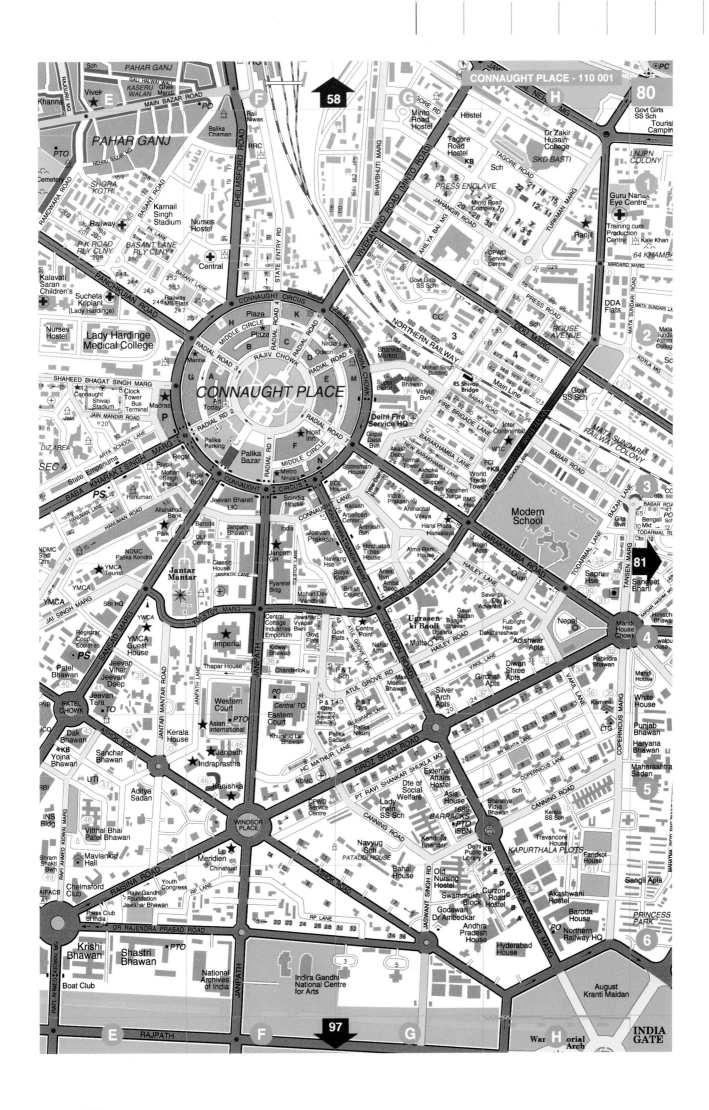

the mapping software, located a software to convert the data into printing files compatible with MAC. Today, nearly all systems are compatible with each other.

Security Clearance

The final maps were sent for security clearance to the Ministry of Defence. Never before had such a detailed map been created, that too on computers by a private firm. It was the first time in India that the latest technology in digital cartography had been used on such a large scale. The project was very capital intensive. We had followed the mapping rules laid down by the government. But still the doubt as to whether we would obtain security clearance remained. Many months passed, reminders were sent, queries raised by the government were clarified. Would we be able to publish the map? This worry gave me many sleepless nights. At last, nine months after submitting the map we heard from the Ministry of Defence. They had no objection to the unrestricted publication of the Eicher City Map of Delhi. We were ecstatic to say the least.

The map was printed and launched in December 1995. It sold out in no time and had to be reprinted at short intervals. It topped the list of bestsellers for many months. Delhiites had taken to the map of their city – our hard work and efforts had been worthwhile. For me, it was a dream come true.

ACKNOWLEDGEMENTS

Survey of India maps are reproduced courtesy the Surveyor General of India.

Other maps and the hand drawn coloured poster "Delhi Through the Ages" are reproduced courtesy Eicher Goodearth Limited.

REFERENCES

Historical Records of the Survey of India.

"A Brief History of the Survey of India 1767–1967", by Lt. Gen. G.C. Agarwal.

"Survey of India through the Ages", by Lt. Gen. S.M. Chadha.

S.M. Chadha

Nitin Rai

Roaming through Delhi

Strolling through Jahanpanah City Forest.

previous page
Chatting by the roadside,
Lajpat Rai Market.

The causeway to Tughluqabad Fort and Ghiyasuddin's tomb.

Yoga session at Lodi Gardens.

Nitin Rai

March of the guards at
Rashtrapati Bhavan.

Life in the courtyard of
Jama Masjid.

Nitin Rai

Remains of the stepped
embankments around the tank,
Surajkund.

Nitin Rai

A peaceful afternoon at
Lodi Gardens.

Harish Yadav has been feeding gulls
on the banks of the Yamuna for the
last forty years.

Eastern verandah of the
Jama Masjid facing the Red Fort.

Nitin Rai

The daily chaos at
Khari Baoli.

A Punjabi family on the roof of their Lajpat Nagar house.

A moment of quiet at Old Delhi Railway Station.

Nitin Rai

Business is brisk in
Sarojini Nagar Market.

The Metropolitan Mall in Gurgaon,
a popular hangout.

Traffic on Rajpath proceeding
towards India Gate.

Jantar Mantar with high-rises
in the background.

Nitin Rai

Festivities at the dargah of
Nizamuddin Awliya.

overleaf
A view of the Shish Gumbad at
Lodi Gardens.

Nitin Rai

Index